A Short History of the Holy Land

Second Edition
2021

Published by CJM Works

ISBN 978-0-9568392-3-7

Printed and bound by CPI Group (UK) Ltd, Croydon, CR0 4YY

About the Author

Chris Mottershead qualified initially as a teacher of Rural Science and later took a Diploma in the Teaching of Religious Education.

From 1986-1990 he was Deputy Headteacher of the Anglican International School, Jerusalem. This school is part of the Church's Ministry among the Jewish People and was originally a mission hospital. It caters for international students from all over the world, and some local students.

From 2000-2005 he was Principal of Tabeetha School in Jaffa. This school is part of the work of the Church of Scotland's World Mission Council. It caters in the main for the local Arab population with some international students.

Both these schools had Christian, Jewish and Arab staff as well as at least some students from all three backgrounds. His time overseas included the First and Second Intifadas and the Second Gulf War. The author has seen some of the suffering resulting from these situations but also experienced some of the local initiatives for reconciliation.

This book aims only to provide an initial overview of the topic after which the reader can pursue areas of particular interest.

Chapters

Maps and Charts

Appendix

Photographs

Front cover – view looking toward the City of David, Jerusalem, taken from St. Peter in Galicantu 2015. Back cover – Yehudiot waterfall, Lower Golan 2020. Both photographs taken by the author.

THE MIDDLE EAST

Location Guide - no fixed date

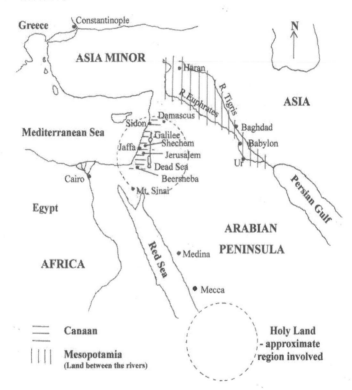

Abram is thought to have travelled in a north-westerly direction from Ur to Haran, then south west into Canaan. The direct route from Ur to Canaan would have been very difficult regarding water sources.

1. Origins

The title 'Holy Land' calls for an account of how certain major religions came to be involved in the region. It also serves to designate an area of land without resorting to specific names such as Palestine or Israel, whose boundaries have varied over the years. At the same time, it has to be acknowledged that surrounding regions and powers further afield, including major powers, have influenced what has happened in the Holy Land. Even its geographical position, at the junction of three continents, has incurred special attention. One could amend the name to 'Not So Holy Land', in order to express concern, even frustration, at the ongoing difficulties in resolving what is simply referred to out there as 'The Situation'.

Dealing with the religions initially, we need to go back approximately four thousand years to the time when an elderly man named Abram made a big decision about where to live. His story features in the scriptures of Judaism, Christianity and Islam. He is respected by all three religions, and is considered to be the founder of Judaism, the first of the three chronologically speaking, so he makes a suitable starting point.

According to the Jewish scriptures, God chose to make a deal, or covenant, with Abram. If he would uproot his family from their home in Ur, and travel to a new land, God would make him father of a nation and a blessing to all nations. Childless at that time, Abram accepted and moved out, ending up in Canaan on the coast of the Mediterranean Sea.

Ten years on, and no child had been born to Abram and his wife Sarai, so they pursued a local custom. Because of the importance attached to having a male heir, the husband was permitted to have a child by one of the handmaids. As a result, their maid Hagar fell pregnant. Sarai became jealous and expelled her, but the Scriptures relate how an angel came to the rescue and restored Hagar to the family home. Abram was eighty-six when Hagar bore him a son named Ishmael.

Thirteen years later, God reaffirmed his covenant with Abram, re-naming him 'Abraham', meaning 'father of a multitude, and Sarai was re-named Sarah. At the same time God promised Abraham the land, and required the introduction of circumcision as a seal of the covenant. Soon afterwards the aged Sarah bore Abraham a son, whom they named Isaac. Problems between her and Hagar then resurfaced, leading to the maid's expulsion along with Ishmael. This time God rescued them and they settled to the south in Paran, in the region of Sinai, with the promise that Ishmael would become the father of a great nation.

Even at this early stage then, Abraham had two lines of promised descendants, both to become 'multitudes', one through Ishmael and the other through Isaac.

Following Isaac's line to begin with, there was an occasion when God tested Abraham by asking that he offer back his son Isaac by way of a sacrifice. Abraham was willing but did not have to go through with it because an angel intervened and a ram was offered on the altar instead. God then again reaffirmed his covenant with Abraham.

The place to which Abraham was sent by God to sacrifice Isaac is significant. It was three days journey from where he lived, to the south, to reach the allotted site at Mt. Moriah. This 'high place' is where Jerusalem is situated today. It is one of the highest peaks in the region, at around 750 metres above sea level. The traditional place of the sacrifice is a large flat rock, a site which therefore ties Jerusalem to the earliest events in Jewish history.

According to the Jewish Scriptures, the covenant was passed on from Abraham to Isaac and then to one of his sons, Jacob. After an encounter with an angel, Jacob's name was changed to Israel, meaning 'God wrestler' or 'one who contends with God'. He had twelve sons, his favourite, Joseph, being the firstborn of his first love, Rachel. Rejected by his jealous brothers, Joseph ended up as a slave in Egypt but eventually rose to a very senior position. When a severe famine hit the region Egypt was prepared, thanks to Joseph. His brothers came in search of food, and Joseph eventually made himself known to them and facilitated their migration from Canaan to join him in Egypt. The estimated date for this move is around 1700 BCE.

The whole family numbered seventy persons when it arrived in Goshen, Egypt. They flourished there for four centuries, until they were so numerous that the Egyptian Pharaoh at the time feared they might side with his enemies against him, so he enslaved them. Known as Hebrews, after the language they spoke, or Israelites, because of their line of descent, they retained their allegiance to the God of the covenant. So, when they cried out for help, God sent a man named Moses to rescue them. After a series of ten plagues and an escape through the Red (or Reed) Sea, a vast number of people were freed. This escape from slavery is still celebrated every year at the Jewish Passover festival.

Moses led them to Mt. Sinai where God gave him the Law (Torah) by which the people were to live. It included the Ten Commandments, written on stone tablets and kept in a specially constructed Ark. This was located in the Tabernacle, a large tent-like structure in which the sacrifices laid out in the Law were performed, and which travelled with them. The covenant originally made between God and Abraham was now between God and his people – the descendants of Israel. If they would follow him and obey his commandments, he would be their God and care for them. The religion which later became known as Judaism was thus established, but where were they to live?

Under Moses' leadership they headed towards Canaan, the land promised to Abraham, which they had left over four hundred years previously. Fearful of the strength of the inhabitants of Canaan, they declined their first opportunity to invade. Consequently, they wandered through the wilderness for many years, until a new generation took up the challenge afresh. They eventually reached the east bank of the River Jordan, opposite Canaan, where Moses died and Joshua took over in 1260 BCE.

So many thousands of people had come out of Egypt, that there was no question of quietly settling back into Canaan, which was a collection of city states at that time. Joshua therefore crossed the Jordan and began a military campaign. This began with the fall of fortress Jericho and continued until Joshua was able to allocate land to the twelve tribes. The list of twelve matches the twelve sons of Israel (Jacob), except that the priestly tribe of Levi had no land while the tribes descended from Joseph's two sons, Ephraim and Manasseh, both had an allocation. The Levites were given towns throughout the twelve allocations. Although the whole area was apportioned, this did not mean that all the local tribes had been driven out.

The military campaign was renewed after Joshua's death, under a succession of leaders known as 'Judges'. Under this regime the Israelites had only limited success, so they demanded a king – to be like all the local tribes. The prophet Samuel anointed Saul as the first King of Israel in 1025 BCE. He had some military success before being killed in battle and was succeeded by David. At first David ruled only Judah, consisting of the tribe of that name plus the Benjaminites, who had been severely depleted in numbers after a serious dispute with the other tribes. A few years later, he was invited to become king over all the tribes of Israel.

Desiring to unite the ten northern tribes with Judah in the south, David sought a capital city somewhere between the two. Jerusalem was the ideal choice but it was still occupied by the Jebusite tribe. However, some of David's soldiers gained access via a water tunnel and captured the city with ease. David took up residence there in order to make Jerusalem the political, as well as geographical, centre of Israel. He went further and made Jerusalem the religious centre of the country by bringing the Ark, symbolising the people's covenant with God since Sinai, into the city.

David also wanted to build a temple but had too much blood on his hands as a warrior, according to God's message delivered to him by the prophet Nathan. David achieved considerable success against the local and surrounding tribes, thereby enlarging the Kingdom of Israel and paving the way for a time of peace and prosperity. His achievements led him to be recognised as Israel's greatest king, and the model for a 'Messiah' (deliverer) type of figure in later generations. The extent of the land of Israel under his rule also became the ideal for some Jewish people down to the present day.

David's son Solomon succeeded him and built the first Temple in Jerusalem between 960 and 952 BCE. The Ark was placed in the Holy of Holies, the innermost part of the Temple, and the sacrificial system thus became centralised in the capital city. Significantly, the Temple and its courtyards embraced Mt. Moriah, including the place where Abraham offered Isaac. The construction of this first permanent Temple confirmed Jerusalem as the prime holy site for what would become known as the Jewish faith.

Solomon developed trade and commerce, bringing prosperity to the land. But as the country's wealth grew, so did the number of Solomon's wives, some of whom he married to cement alliances with surrounding nations. According to the Jewish Scriptures, his conceding to their requests for altars to foreign gods led to a divided kingdom after his death. His son Rehoboam, based in Jerusalem, retained the two southern tribes of Judah and Benjamin. The other ten tribes re-formed the northern kingdom of Israel under Jeroboam, based at Shechem. Early in Rehoboam's reign, Jerusalem was attacked by Shishak, King of Egypt. Shishak carried off most of the Temple treasures, but Rehoboam survived.

The northern kingdom had a succession of kings, mostly inadequate, until it fell to the Assyrians, invading from the north in 721 BCE. From this time onwards the ten tribes began to assimilate

EARLY SETTLEMENT of the TWELVE TRIBES

BOLD CAPITALS = **Tribes of Israel**

Italics = *Other Tribes*

The members of the priestly tribe of Levi were allocated towns within the areas allocated to the other tribes. Joseph's two sons, Ephraim and Manasseh were both allocated land.

or disperse, to the extent that they are now referred to as 'The Ten Lost Tribes of Israel'. The Assyrians deported some Israelites and settled people from the east in their place. Being in the region known as Samaria, this settlement, with accompanying intermarriage, produced the race known as the Samaritans.

The southern kingdom successfully resisted the Assyrians and lasted another 150 years, until the Babylonian invasion led by Nebuchadnezzar. The people of Judah refused to believe prophets like Jeremiah, who predicted the fall of Jerusalem. But fall it did, in 586 BCE, with the city walls and the Temple destroyed. All but the poorest people were taken into captivity; a few being left behind to work the land.

Summary: The man Abraham was the forefather of the Israelite race which established a nation in the region of Canaan. Led by Judges, then Kings, they established their own religion with a central Temple in their capital city of Jerusalem. Invasions resulted in many of the tribes of Israel being lost, but two were taken into exile.

****

2. Judaism

Throughout their exile in Babylon the people strove to maintain their religious identity. It was during this time that they became known as 'Jews' – from the tribal name Judah (Yehuda in Hebrew). Given that the ten northern tribes had seriously declined since the Assyrian invasion, and that the tribe of Benjamin was few in number, the tribe of Judah was the only remaining tribe of any size. Therefore, the people's religion can be referred to as 'Judaism' from this point in time. There were Levites amongst them because this, the priestly tribe, had been allocated towns throughout all the other tribes of Israel originally.

Within fifty years of the beginning of the Jewish exile, the Medes and Persians ousted the Babylonians and decreed that all exiled peoples may return to their homeland. The first Jewish group to do so faced a daunting task. Led by Zerubbabel they went to Jerusalem and rebuilt the altar, and then a new temple. This 'Second Temple' was much less impressive than Solomon's building, but the sacrificial system was back in operation. There was opposition to their return from some local tribes, including Arabs and Samaritans. When the scribe Ezra arrived in Jerusalem, he prohibited inter-marriage with local tribes in order to maintain the Jewish identity that had survived the exile. Nehemiah returned to rebuild the walls of Jerusalem and also faced local opposition. However, as with Zerubbabel, appeals to the Mede and Persian authorities brought sufficient backing to overcome this opposition and complete the task.

The returning remnant of the tribe of Judah re-established themselves in and around Jerusalem. However, there was no 'Kingdom of Israel' because the region remained under the control of the Empire of the Medes and Persians. There a Samaritan approach to the Jews regarding a joint effort in the rebuilding, but this was rejected because of the Samaritan's history of inter-marriage and their differing rites of worship. The fate of the peasant farmers left behind by the Babylonians fifty years previously is unclear, but some of them are thought to have fled to Egypt.

By the fourth century BCE, Judaism was to be found in the region of Judea, with Jerusalem and its Temple as the prime holy site. There were Arab and other tribes in the surrounding regions, but no Christianity or Islam as yet. Other religions at the time were based mainly on tribal gods.

The next major change was the displacement of the Medes and Persians by the Greeks, who captured Jerusalem and Judea in 332 BCE. Their all-conquering military leader, Alexander the Great, died only nine years later, leaving the Middle East to his generals. Seleucus received Syria in the north, while Ptolemy received Egypt to the south. The land in the middle, including Judea and Jerusalem, came under Ptolemy's control initially. As time went on, the Seleucids became more powerful and took control of the whole area in 198 BCE.

'Hellenisation' - the adoption of the Greek way of life - was resisted by the Jewish people in order to preserve their identity and worship of one God. They opted out of certain public festivals for example. It was during this period that the Jewish religious 'Pharisee' movement arose to help combat the Greek influence. The Jewish reaction was not appreciated, and gave rise to the concept of 'anti-semitism', though that specific word was not used at the time.

In 167 BCE, matters came to a head when the Seleucid leader Antiochus Epiphanes deliberately defiled the Jewish Temple as part of an ongoing attempt to suppress the Jewish religion. This sparked a successful Jewish revolt led by Judas Maccabeus of the Hasmonean family. Jerusalem was liberated and the Temple was purified – an event remembered in the Jewish festival of Hannukah. The Maccabean family ruled Judea until 63 BCE when the Roman general Pompey occupied Jerusalem. He added the region to the Roman province of Syria, but allowed the Maccabees to continue their rule as a vassal state of Rome. In 38 BCE the Romans took full control and appointed the partly Jewish Herod as King of Judea. Hoping to gain popularity, Herod set about renovating the Jewish Temple and enlarging the Temple Mount. After his death in 4 BCE the kingdom was divided between three of his sons. Archelaus received Judea and Samaria but was not up to the task. After six years he was replaced by the first in a series of Roman Procurators, who were subject to the governor of the Roman province of Syria.

Having referred to Arab tribes in this chapter, it is time to pick up the line of Ishmael and give some idea of their origins. The chart on page 17 offers a summary.

Before Abraham even, both Arabs and Jews trace their origins to Noah's son, Shem - hence the term 'Semitic' derived from 'Shemite'. Note that this name can apply to both races. Although more research is needed on this topic, it appears that there is more than one line of Arab descent from this point.

One major group trace their family back to Shem's sons Aram and Aphaxad. One of this line was a man named Joktan. According to tradition, the term 'Arab' came from the town of Araba on the eastern coast of the Red Sea, named after Joktan's son Ya'rab, who settled there. This line established an early centre of civilisation in the South Arabian Peninsula.

A second major group of Arabs trace their line from Abraham's son Ishmael. Muslims believe Ishmael learned Arabic, therefore the term 'Arabised' is sometimes used to describe this group. Ishmael had twelve sons, from whom derive the twelve tribes of Northern Arabia. This fulfilled God's promise to his mother Hagar, after her expulsion by Sarai, that her son would have a multitude of descendants.

There is also a smaller Arab group descending from Abraham's marriage to Keturah. Their sons Medan and Midian are thought to be the forefathers of the Desert Bedouin.

An approximate guide to the origins of Arabs and Jews

(straight line = one generation, dotted line = several)

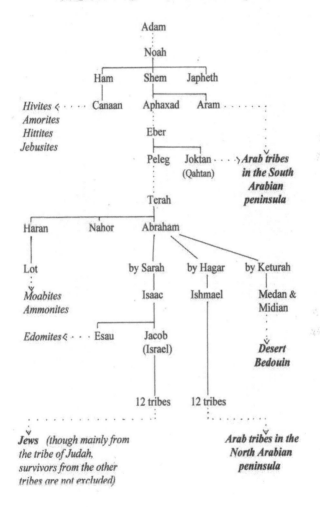

When considering the origins of tribes in general, it is worth bearing in mind that their composition is likely to have been affected in varying degrees by war, migration and inter-marriage, especially over a long period of time.

Summary: The Israelite religion became known as Judaism from the time in exile. When they were allowed to return to Judea they built a new temple in Jerusalem. They remained under the authority of the dominant empire of the day apart from a period when they regained control over Jerusalem.

******

3. Add Christianity

Under Roman rule the Jewish people were able to worship and offer sacrifices in the Temple. They had a council - the Sanhedrin - consisting of Pharisees and the more traditional Sadduccees. The latter group had replaced the High Priestly lineage after the Maccabean revolt and thereafter filled the High Priest position. Despite the apparent religious freedom, there remained a strong hope for a 'messiah', someone anointed as king, who would deliver them from the Roman occupation. The most popular idea of a messiah was a King David type of figure, but a very different type of leader appeared on the scene instead.

A rabbi named Jesus came from Nazareth, preaching the good news of the coming of the 'Kingdom of God (or Heaven)'. He began his ministry in Galilee and ended up riding into Jerusalem on a donkey, hailed by cheering crowds as their Messiah, Son of David. His teaching was popular with the people, but a serious challenge to the Pharisees, particularly his claim to be the Son of God. His cleansing the Temple of traders and money-changers threatened the Sadduccees, who controlled both of those operations. As a result, these two parties endeavoured to remove this challenge to their authority by presenting Jesus to the Romans as a threat to peace. The Roman Procurator at the time, Pontius Pilate, eventually acceded to their demands and had Jesus crucified outside Jerusalem. The date was probably 33 CE, according to the calendar based on the birth of Jesus Christ. The Jewish calendar recognises no such break.

This was not the end of the story, however, because Jesus' followers claimed he rose from the dead on the third day after his crucifixion. He appeared to many of them during the next forty days, before ascending to his Father in heaven. After the Jewish festival of Pentecost, his disciples, filled with God's Holy Spirit, picked up where he left off, and large numbers of Jews became followers of

'The Way'. Later, their message was taken to non-Jews (Gentiles) and the nickname 'Christians' – followers of the Christ (anointed one) – was given, thereby establishing a new religion.

For Christians, the Messiah is Jesus of Nazareth; for most Jews the Messiah is still to come. Christianity clearly has its roots in Judaism - Jesus and most of his early followers being Jewish. The Jewish Tanakh scriptures would become the Christian Old Testament – the same books only in a different arrangement. The covenant for Jews is between God and his people, and requires observance of the Law as given to Moses and applied by their religious authorities. For Christians, God's covenant becomes a personal relationship. This leads to a further divergence. For Jews, there is the sacrificial system for the atonement (ransom payment) of wrongdoing or 'sin'. This was centralised at the Temple in Jerusalem, but local priests could also perform the necessary ceremonies. For Christians, Christ's death on the cross was a once and for all sacrifice for people's sins. It was then only necessary for a person to accept this by faith, thereby removing the need for the sacrificial system practised in Judaism.

Jerusalem itself gained further importance with the advent of Christianity. It was now the city where the Christian Saviour came to fulfil his destiny. The sites of his crucifixion and resurrection were there, and pilgrims would want to visit Jerusalem in the years to come. The holiest city of Judaism was now also the holiest city of Christianity.

Many of Jesus' senior disciples based themselves in Jerusalem, while others were sent abroad to spread the 'gospel' – the good news of Jesus Christ. Persecution by the Jewish religious authorities helped to spread the new faith, as believers escaped or fled to new places. One of their main persecutors, Saul of Tarsus, was converted on the road to Damascus. He was re-named Paul, and he became an important missionary around the Eastern Mediterranean region, establishing groups of believers or 'churches' in several towns and countries.

Jewish Tanakh (Bible)

Torah
1.Genesis
2.Exodus
3.Leviticus
4.Numbers
5.Deuteronomy

Prophets	Later, Minor
Early	13.Hosea
6.Joshua	13.Joel
7.Judges	13.Amos
8.Samuel	13.Obadiah
9.Kings	13.Jonah
	13.Micah
Later, Major	13.Nahum
10.Isaiah	13.Habakkuk
11.Jeremiah	13.Zephaniah
12.Ezekiel	13. Haggai
	13 Zechariah
	13.Malachi

Writings
14.Psalms
15.Proverbs
16.Job
17.Song of Solomon
18.Ruth
19.Lamentations
20.Ecclesiastes
21.Esther
22.Daniel
23.Ezra & Nehemiah
24.Chronicles

Twenty-four books in total, as indicated by the numbering.

Christian Old Testament

1. Genesis
2. Exodus
3. Leviticus
4. Numbers
5. Deuteronomy
6. Joshua
7. Judges
8. Ruth
9. I Samuel
10.II Samuel
11.I Kings
12.II Kings
13.I Chronicles
14.II Chronicles
15.Ezra
16.Nehemiah
17.Esther
18.Job
19.Psalms
20.Proverbs
21.Ecclesiastes
22.Song of Solomon
23.Isaiah
24.Jeremiah
25.Lamentations
26.Ezekiel
27.Daniel
28.Hosea
29.Joel
30.Amos
31.Obadiah

32.Jonah	36.Zephaniah
33.Micah	37.Haggai
34.Nahum	38.Zechariah
35.Habakkuk.	39.Malachi

Thirty-nine books in total.

While Christianity was spreading rapidly, the Jewish urge to be rid of the Roman occupation erupted in the revolt of 66 CE. It took the Romans four years to put down this uprising, culminating in the fall of Jerusalem and the burning down of the Temple. With it went the Jewish sacrificial system. The severity of the defeat caused many Jews to move to safer regions, thereby initiating the 'Diaspora' - a forced or voluntary migration away from their homeland.

There was one final 'military' messiah figure, Simon bar Kochba, whose revolt in 132 CE briefly restored the Temple services. Three years later he was defeated by the Roman Emperor Hadrian. He flattened Jerusalem and built a new city on the site, naming it 'Aelia Capitolina', with a temple to Jupiter in place of the Jewish Temple. The Romans were determined to erase the Jewish people and their capital city from the map altogether, so Hadrian renamed the region of Judea 'Syria Palestina'. The latter word comes from the tribal name 'Philistine', deliberately chosen because that tribe was an old enemy of Israel. The new name indicates that the land was considered to be part of greater Syria.

If 70 CE marked the beginning of the Jewish Diaspora, 135 CE gave it added impetus. Hadrian banned the Jews from even living in Aelia Capitolina and the surrounding areas. However, enough rabbis survived elsewhere, especially to the north - in Tiberius for example. In the absence of the Temple and its associated practices, they established 'Rabbinic Judaism', by which they taught and interpreted the Law given to Moses at Sinai. The Jewish presence in the land promised to Abram was considerably depleted for many centuries to come. For years a Roman garrison prevented them from entering their old capital while Gentiles took over several Jewish towns. There was some respite in the third century CE, when they were granted access to Aelia Capitolina once a year. This allowed them to mourn at what remained of the western wall of the Temple – hence the name 'Wailing Wall'.

Meanwhile, Christianity was spreading, despite persecution from several Roman emperors. Then, in 312 CE, the Emperor Constantine was converted, and a few years later he made Christianity a legal religion. He also established the city of Constantinople, (where Istanbul is today), as capital of the eastern half of the Roman Empire. While the west was to fall to the Goths, the east resisted the Persian threat and so maintained its control over the Middle East for another three centuries.

Those centuries saw Christianity continue to grow. The basic creeds and canon of scripture were established. Twenty-seven books relating the life of Jesus and his apostles, plus certain letters (epistles), made up the New Testament. This was added to the Old Testament (Jewish Tanakh) to produce the Christian Bible. A group of believers in any given place was called a 'church', a name which was also applied to the buildings they could now safely erect as places in which to meet and worship. The name Aelia Capitolina reverted to Jerusalem, where the Holy Sepulchre church, traditionally covering the site of Christ's death and resurrection, was completed in 335 CE under Constantine's instruction. That church is a major holy site to this day. A Christian calendar was established, based on the birth year of Jesus Christ.

The new faith flourished among Arab tribes, and a large number of churches appeared. For them the Christian faith identified with Abraham's personal walk with God, and did away with idols and legalism.

The region now contained the key Christian sites, including places Jesus visited before he came to Jerusalem. The abundance of sites, and Jerusalem in particular, attracted the first Christian pilgrims to what became known as 'The Holy Land'. The demise of the Roman Empire in the west actually led some Christians to move eastwards and re-settle in The Holy Land.

Syria Palestina prospered during this 'Byzantine' period. Rabbinic Judaism was not dormant either, as evidenced by the rabbis' completion of the Talmud. This is a written account of what Jews believe was the oral law given to Moses at Sinai, (in addition to the written law), along with its meaning and application. Judaism did come under increasing pressure from laws made by the Christian Roman Empire, but although their numbers were further reduced by the end of the sixth century, they were still present in the land.

Summary: The teachings of a Jewish Rabbi from Nazareth led to a new sect of Judaism, which grew into the separate religion of Christianity. Meanwhile, the dispersal of the Jewish people after their unsuccessful revolt against the Romans and loss of their Temple, led to their being guided by Rabbinic teachings instead of the sacrificial system. The Holy Land, and Jerusalem in particular, now had key sites pertaining to Judaism and Christianity. The region included both Jewish and Arab people.

****

4. Add Islam

It was towards the end of the sixth century that the third major religion emerged in the Middle East. The man Muhammad, born in Mecca in 570 CE, belonged to an idol worshipping tribe, but he was aware of the Christian and Jewish faiths through his work on merchant caravans. At the age of forty he began receiving visions from the Angel Gabriel, which led him to encourage his people to follow 'the one true God'. Opposition from those who controlled the Meccan shrines forced him to move to Medina in 622 CE, (see map on page 6) where he established a community based on his teachings. His followers were called 'Muslim', meaning 'one who submits (to God)'. His teachings were written down, in Arabic, in a holy book known as the Qur'an.

The start of the Medina community marked the beginning of the Muslim calendar and the religion of Islam – a word meaning 'submission'. During his time at Medina, Muhammad came into conflict with local Jewish tribes, one of which was forcibly removed. This contributed to the emerging rift between Muslims and Jews, but there was some common ground. The Qur'an refers to Noah, Abraham and other Jewish figures as prophets, also to Jesus from the Christian New Testament. However, there are crucial differences, for example Muslims believe Abraham offered Ishmael, not Isaac, and at a site near Mecca not on Mt. Moriah, and that salvation is dependent on the individual's good deeds outweighing bad deeds come judgement day.

Muhammad captured Mecca, where the Ka'aba shrine, built by Abraham and Ishmael according to the Qu'ran, became the House of God. Prayers were said facing this shrine and Mecca became the central site of the Muslim pilgrimage. Muhammad died in 632 CE without a male heir and a succession of leaders known as 'caliphs'

The Early Caliphate of Islam

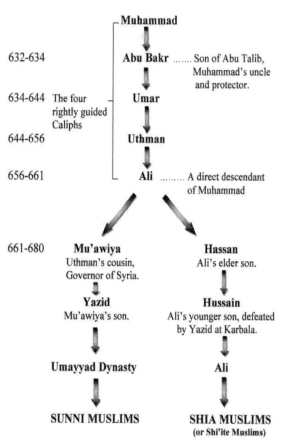

Muhammad

632-634   Abu Bakr .... Son of Abu Talib,
Muhammad's uncle
and protector.

634-644   The four   Umar
rightly guided
Caliphs

644-656   Uthman

656-661   Ali .... A direct descendant
of Muhammad

661-680   **Mu'awiya**   **Hassan**
Uthman's cousin,   Ali's elder son.
Governor of Syria.

Yazid   **Hussain**
Mu'awiya's son.   Ali's younger son, defeated
by Yazid at Karbala.

Umayyad Dynasty   **Ali**

SUNNI MUSLIMS   **SHIA MUSLIMS**
                      (or Shi'ite Muslims)

The **Qu'ran**, divided into 114 surahs (like chapters) is the written record of Muhammad's visions. The **Sunnah** is the oral tradition which arose outside of the Qu'ran. The **Hadith** is a multi-volume written record of over seven thousand sayings of Muhammad. **Shariah Law** is the legal framework based on the above, with modern day application, based on concensus, and covering all aspects of life.

ensued, but there was a major division after the fourth one. The Shia Muslims maintained that the leadership should be passed down via direct descendants of the prophet Muhammad, while the Sunni Muslims accepted strong leaders regardless of their line of descent.

Islam united the Arab tribes as never before. In 634 CE, two years after Muhammad's death, they began a conquest which established an empire stretching from Spain (via North Africa) to the borders of China, in less than a century. The Romans were removed from Syria Palestina - Jerusalem surrendering to Caliph Umar in 638 CE. Jerusalem was renamed 'Al Quds', and Syria Palestina became 'Filastin' or Palestine, with its capital at Ramla.

After the fourth caliph, the Sunni Umayyad family established the first Islamic dynasty, with its capital at Damascus. As Islam spread, Arabic replaced most other languages. Jews and Christians were tolerated as 'People of the Book', and were offered protected (dhimmi) status in return for tax payments, but many of them still converted to Islam.

Islam established its claim to Jerusalem/Al Quds, when Caliph Abd al-Malik erected the Dome of the Rock on the Temple Mount in 691 CE, followed by the Al-Aksa Mosque, nearby, a few years later. The 'rock' under the beautiful golden dome is the Jewish site for the sacrifice of Isaac, but for Muslims it is the site to which Muhammad journeyed one night from Mecca, on his steed Buraq. From the rock he ascended to the seventh heaven, meeting with several prophets en route, before returning to Mecca the same night. This event signifies a transfer of authority from Isaac's line to Ishmael's; from Judaism and Christianity to Islam. At the same time, Jerusalem/Al Quds became the third holiest city in Islam, after Mecca and Medina. Pictures can be seen in Jerusalem today, depicting Jerusalem's Dome of the Rock alongside the Ka'aba in Mecca. This is an important point in the consideration of the Holy Land in present times.

In 750 CE the Abbasid Muslims ousted the Umayyads and the capital was moved to Baghdad. Under their caliphate, learning and culture flourished, giving rise to the period known as the 'Golden Age of Islam'. However, as the empire grew there came a time when they had to train Turkish slave boys from Central Asia as soldiers in order to maintain the numbers in their army. In time, these 'Mamelukes' became so proficient that in 861 CE they were able to stage a coup and establish a military dictatorship. Their initial period in power did not last long, but they did control Palestine for a time, and they would reappear later.

As the Islamic period proceeded through different phases, the Muslims became the majority group in Palestine. At the same time, they became generally less tolerant of the remaining Christian and Jewish communities which had not converted. However, they did allow Jews to reside again in Jerusalem, which then replaced Tiberius as their centre of learning. The Jews themselves were concentrating their numbers in the towns to help maintain their identity. The reduced tolerance of Christians by the Muslims, especially regarding the holy sites and therefore pilgrimage, very significantly aroused support from Europe.

Late in the eleventh century, the most powerful Muslims, the Seljuk Turks, who originated in Central Asia, posed a serious threat to the Eastern Christian Byzantine Empire. This caused Emperor Alexius Comnenus to turn to Pope Urban II and Western Christians, for help. He cited the hardships for Christians living under Islam in the Holy Land, and for pilgrims trying to visit the holy sites. In response, Urban called for a holy war combined with a pilgrimage, to rescue the Holy Land from the Muslims. Tax incentives and indulgences were offered, the latter guaranteeing the soldiers entry into heaven for joining what became known as the 'Crusades'.

The First Crusade travelled overland via Constantinople. The Crusaders went on from there to capture Jerusalem in 1099. They set up small Crusader states at Edessa, Antioch, Tripoli and Jerusalem. The Muslim recapture of Edessa in 1144 precipitated the Second Crusade, which failed to regain it. Improved Muslim unity enabled them to conduct their own holy war, culminating in Saladin's defeat of the Crusaders at Hattin in 1187. He then re-captured Jerusalem, restoring its Arabic name, Al-Quds, and over-ran the Crusader lands. A Third Crusade recovered some of the land but not Jerusalem.

Further Crusades followed, resulting in a steady stream of soldiers and pilgrims. The coastal town of Acre became the Crusader capital. Jerusalem was regained by negotiation for a short time, but the Muslims retook it and Louis IX's Crusade failed to win it back. After this, the Mamelukes re-emerged and replaced Saladin's brief dynasty. In the ensuing years they steadily overcame the Crusader settlements, removing them from the Middle East (except for Cyprus) by taking Acre in 1291.

The final expulsion of the Christian invaders was a significant triumph for Islam as the leading faith in the region. Popes were already diverting their Crusades towards European heretics, while some Christian leaders argued in favour of peaceful missions to convert the Muslims. The Crusades had focussed Muslim attention on Jerusalem, increasing its religious importance to Islam. For the Jews the Crusades remain a bad memory even today because many Jewish communities, in Europe as well as in the Holy land, suffered at the hands of the Crusaders.

While dealing with the final Crusades, the Muslims also faced invaders from the east. The Mongols defeated the Seljuk Turks and captured Baghdad in 1258. In response, the Mamelukes marched out of Egypt and defeated the Mongols at Ain Jalout in Palestine's Jezreel Valley. This decisive victory kept the Middle East in Muslim hands. The site of the battle is just one example of how the Holy Land was often caught between two major powers.

The Mamelukes took control but their own military code prevented them from establishing a dynasty, so their rulers (sultans) were regularly displaced by stronger rivals. This changed early in the fourteenth century, when the Turkish warrior prince Osman founded the Ottoman dynasty. In the following decades his Sunni Muslims expanded westwards into Europe, as well as eastwards. In 1453 they captured Constantinople, thereby removing what remained of the Byzantine Empire and marking the final collapse of non-Muslim power in the Middle–East. Further to the east they steadily overcame the Shia Muslim Persians, while in Egypt they gained power over the Mamelukes, though allowing them to rule under their control.

Most of the Middle East therefore became part of the Ottoman Empire. For Palestine this dated from 1517, and was to last for exactly four hundred years. The sultans held the keys to Mecca and the responsibility of 'Protector of the Holy Places'. They also received the title 'Caliph of Islam' and resided in Istanbul, (previously Constantinople). Leadership of the Muslim world thus passed from Arabs to Turks. The Ottomans administered Palestine as part of Greater Syria, using mainly local people as civil servants. Jerusalem was their capital, and Sultan Sulieman re-built the city walls. However, they showed little interest in colonising the rest of the country and left it to decline.

Summary: The religion of Islam began in Arabia and established an empire which ruled the Middle East for several centuries, apart from a period when Christian Crusaders controlled the Holy Land. Jerusalem became the third holiest city for Muslims. The Muslim Ottoman Turks took over from the Arab dynasties and held control of the Holy Land into the modern age.

Note that the conquering Arab Muslims used the name 'Palestine', derived from the Roman name Syria Palestina, which Emperor Hadrian gave to Judea in 135 CE. They re-named Jerusalem 'Al Quds'.

****

5. European Interest

Not a great deal happened in the Holy Land under Ottoman rule until the nineteenth century, when two outside influences began to take effect. The first was geo-political in nature. Several European countries had been making good progress through trade and commerce, thereby developing into major powers. The Middle East provided the most direct overland route to India and the Far East, so the British and the Dutch, for example, had established a naval presence in the Eastern Mediterranean by 1800, with their trade links in mind. The French then took a more direct interest in the region.

Napoleon landed in Egypt in 1798 and defeated a Mameluke army. The Ottoman Sultan reacted by allying himself with Britain and Russia in order to stop the French as they marched along the coast into the Holy Land, via Jaffa, as far as Acre. Napoleon had even promised to restore the Jews to Jerusalem and rebuild their Temple if they would help him conquer Palestine. However, they chose to maintain their allegiance to the Ottomans and so Napoleon's campaign failed. Never-the-less, European interest in the Middle East had been very much awakened.

This interest was not only geo-political. The second influence was from a religious source. The previous century's religious revival in Britain, with some earlier Puritan influence, had led to a more literal interpretation of the Bible by many Christians. One outcome of this was the belief that the Jewish people must be restored to the biblical land of Israel and recognise Jesus Christ as their Messiah, before his second coming could take place. This belief had practical results, for example the London Society for Promoting Christianity Amongst the Jews, formed in 1809. By 1822 this organisation had started a mission in Jerusalem itself. Politicians such as Lord Shaftesbury and William Wilberforce supported this religious movement, which therefore began to influence Britain's political stance on the Middle-East. This particular mission was one of many which were established in the Holy Land during the nineteenth century.

The geo-political and religious interest from Europe received a boost from within the Middle East itself when Muhammad (or Mehmet) Ali, an Ottoman commander, who was a native of Albania, entered the scene. He was dispatched to Egypt by the Ottoman Sultan to reclaim it after a Mameluke uprising. This he did, in 1811, and by way of reward the Sultan allowed him to retain control of Egypt. Ali went on to reclaim for the Sultan the Muslim holy places, which had been taken over by the radical Muslim Wahabists at the turn of the century. This time the Sultan declined Ali's request for control of Syria as his reward, so Ali took the Sudan instead. Later he moved into Syria on his own initiative, from where he threatened Istanbul itself. The British declined the Sultan's appeal for help, so he turned to the Russians. The British and the French, ever wary of Russian influence, objected and insisted on a Russian withdrawal, plus concessions to Ali by way of control over Syria, which included Palestine - and that is what happened.

Ali was not an Arabic speaker but his son Ibrahim was, so he was given the task of ruling Syria, including Palestine, from 1831 to 1840. Most significantly he and his father were modernisers, promoting non-Muslims where necessary. This was a major development which allowed Christian merchants to develop links with Europe. Furthermore, minority religions were given equal status so, for example, Christian schools were permitted in the region and many clergy went to live in Palestine. The small Jewish population also benefited; synagogues being restored and access granted to the Western (Wailing) Wall. The British established a Consulate in Jerusalem in 1839, the first of the European powers allowed to do so.

Britain then decided it needed to protect its important trade routes through the Ottoman Empire by means of a treaty, which threatened Ali's status. He responded by declaring both Egypt and Syria independent kingdoms, so the Sultan had to persuade the British and other European countries to help him curtail Ali's ambitions. The outcome was the return of Syria to Ottoman rule in 1840, but Ali retained Egypt until his death. Syria, including the Holy Land, may only have been under Ali's control for a few years, but the gateway to a European style modernisation had most definitely been opened – something not necessarily appreciated by the indigenous population at the time. Furthermore, the Europeans ensured that the Sultan continued the process. So, for example, Sultan Abdul Mejid, (1839-61) passed reforms making all citizens equal in law, thereby creating a new legal code, separate from the Muslim Shariah Law applied by Islamic judges.

As soon as the Sultan regained control over Palestine in 1840, Britain's Lord Shaftesbury and others urged the Foreign Minister, Lord Palmerston, to propose the restoration of the Jews to their promised land in large numbers. The Sultan was not interested, but the seed was sown. Britain and Prussia set up a joint bishopric in Jerusalem, with the former choosing the first bishop, Michael Alexander, a Christian of Jewish descent. He reached Jerusalem in 1842, laid the foundation stone for a new church the same year, and saw a hospital opened in 1844. Alexander died before the completion of the first Protestant church in the Middle East, Christ Church Jerusalem, in 1849.

It must be remembered that there were many other Christians, including Arabs, surviving in the land from the early days of the Eastern Church. Most of them were Orthodox, but there were also some Roman Catholics, and the arrival of the European Protestants caused a revival of activity in these two major branches of Christianity. As early as 1850 a dispute broke out between them concerning control of the holy sites in Palestine. Britain and France backed the Turks in preventing the Russians from trying to take authority over all the Orthodox Christians in the Ottoman Empire. This action drew the Turks closer to Europe.

Rabbis led local Jewish opposition to the work of the Protestant missions with some support from Jews overseas. Sir Moses Montefiore and Baron Edmund de Rothschild in particular, helped to improve the situation for the local people by establishing schools, hospitals and agricultural projects. The resulting agricultural colonies raised the question of interaction with the other residents of the land, and as early as 1861 Jewish writer Ahad Ha'am foresaw the possibility of an Arab-Jewish conflict.

Despite their reforms, the Ottomans were unable to match the progress in Europe made through the industrial revolution, free trade and greater resources. To make matters worse, they borrowed heavily from the European countries in order to carry out their reforms, and began to run into serious debt. The cost of building the Suez Canal, completed in 1869, added to their debts, while providing the Europeans with a sea route to India in addition to the existing overland route – all very useful for trade and commerce.

As far as the Holy Land itself was concerned, Jerusalem was still capital of an Ottoman administrative region (a sanjak), covering southern Palestine. The rest of Palestine was covered by two sanjaks, with capitals at Nablus (Shechem) and Acre. One census of this period reported nearly a quarter of a million Arabs in Palestine, consisting mainly of Fellahin peasant farmers and Bedouin nomads. There being much smaller numbers of Christians and Jews, Islam was the dominant way of life. However, a growing Jewish population in Jerusalem had caused an expansion beyond the Old City walls from the 1860s onwards. There was also some Arab immigration into the Holy Land, drawn by an increase in economic activity.

While content to use Jerusalem as an administrative centre, the Ottomans continued to pay little attention to the rest of the land. It was the increasing European influence which improved the economic situation and brought the region into the international system. Products such as olives, fruit (including Jaffa oranges), cotton and wheat, were traded for manufactured goods from Western Europe. As a result, the towns developed a middle class of merchants and businessmen. New laws allowed the wealthy to buy land without having to live on it, so many of them moved to the towns and visited their estates only occasionally. There was enough freedom for the major Arab families to be able to influence the town councils. At the same time, there was a cultural awakening amongst Christian Arabs due to the European influences.

Into this situation there now came the first practical out-workings of Zionism.

Summary: Geo-political and religious interest from major European powers brought changes to the Holy Land during the nineteenth century. The modernising influence initiated by Muhammad Ali during his short rule over Greater Syria encouraged these changes.

****

6. Zionism

British Christians were not the only people interested in seeing the Jews returning to the Middle East. Jewish rabbis such as Alkalai, Kalischer and Kook had advocated the same thing during the nineteenth century. Alkalai, the first to do so, was influenced by the blood libel against the Jews in Damascus in 1840. They were accused of killing a child and using its blood in a ritual. After this, Alkalai reckoned the Jewish people would only be secure in a land of their own. The term 'Zionism' was used by these Jewish pioneers to represent the idea of a large-scale Jewish restoration to their biblical homeland.

Later on, the writings of Hess, Smolenkin, and Pinsker encouraged Russian Jews to form the 'Lovers of Zion' movement, with the idea of maintaining the Jewish identity by restoration to their homeland. But, because they viewed Palestine as a very poor country, difficult to settle in, very few of them emigrated until 1881. In that year a Jewess was implicated in the assassination of Czar Alexander II. This gave the Russian government an excuse to punish the Jewish population for its resistance to integration. Organised riots, known as 'pogroms' were backed up with a number of legal inhibitions against the Jews, who resided in their own area, known as 'The Pale'. As a result, thousands of Jews migrated to Europe and some of them decided that the option of a homeland in Palestine might be worth the hardships of settlement there.

Moses Montefiore and Edmond de Rothschild gave their support to many of those who migrated. Recent Ottoman reforms allowed them to purchase land, often from wealthy Arab landlords, on which they established villages, whose residents farmed the land as co-operatives (moshavs). Because of its fertility, the coastal plain was more important to the settlers than Jerusalem at that time. The 1880s saw a significant number of new settlements there, but as the numbers of settlers grew, so did tensions between them and the local Palestinian peasant farmers. Disputes over purchased land, for example at Petah Tikva in 1886 and Rehovot in 1892 incurred violent protests. As result of this, prominent Arab families in Jerusalem asked the Ottoman Sultan to control both Jewish immigration and land purchases – a request which was to be repeated in the years to come.

This period of Jewish immigration from Russia, spanning 1881-1904, became known as the 'First Aliyah'. The word aliyah specifically relates to the immigration of Jewish people into their homeland of Israel. The numbers were estimated at around thirty thousand; enough to make a serious impact on the local population. It encouraged a call for an international movement for the establishment of a Jewish homeland - a challenge taken up by Theodore Herzl.

Herzl had been influenced by the Russian pogroms in general and the Dreyfus affair in particular. Dreyfus was a French army officer, wrongly convicted of treason because he was Jewish. Although later pardoned, the anti-Semitic demonstrations which accompanied the case convinced Herzl that the Jewish people could never be properly integrated into Europe. The only answer was for them to have their own state, so in 1896 he published his book 'Der Judenstat' (The Jewish State). This created sufficient support for him to convene the First Zionist Congress in Basle the following year.

Western European Jews backed Herzl's political approach, while those in Eastern Europe adopted the more practical approach of actually settling in Palestine. There were also religious Zionists, who wanted a state governed by Jewish law, and cultural Zionists, who wanted a small settlement which would become a cultural centre for worldwide Jewry. A little later would come the social Zionists, influenced by Karl Marx, leading eventually to the agriculturally based communes (kibbutzim) and a socialist state.

Herzl first approached Sultan Hamid for a charter for Jewish settlement in Palestine under German protection. The Sultan declined, fearing it would damage relations with his Arab subjects, and the German Kaiser did not want to get involved for fear of upsetting his relations with the Turks. Herzl then turned to the other major European power in the region – the British. Foreign Secretary Chamberlain suggested East Africa as an alternative homeland and the 1903 Zionist Congress considered the idea. However, its delegates were very much divided over the matter, and the resulting tensions led to Herzl's early death the following year.

Anti-Semitism persisted in Russia, setting off a Second Aliyah from 1905-1913, which brought Social Zionism to the fore. Pioneers such as David Ben Gurion decreed that the Jewish people would be redeemed through productive labour rather than by any religious means. This group drew money from the Jewish National Fund to purchase land from wealthy Arab families, but they had to work hard to cultivate the land they acquired. The fund originated in 1901 with the express purpose of buying land in Palestine for Jewish settlement.

Figures vary, but another thirty thousand or so are thought to have arrived in Palestine during the Second Aliyah. Added to a similar number in the First Aliyah, this gave the existing Arab residents even more cause for concern. Arab culture and Islamic values began to be threatened, not only by the Jewish influx, but by the European influences which came with them. In addition, Christian missionaries and western tourists were coming to the Holy Land in increasing numbers. Western powers were establishing a keen interest in the region, with regard to both trade routes and holy sites.

This situation resulted in the first signs of Arab nationalism, reinforced by the changes they faced from their Ottoman rulers. A new, educated Turkish middle-class had set up a Committee of Union and Progress, aimed at uniting the different races within the empire. This led to the Young Turks Revolution, which replaced the Sultan's despotism with a constitutional monarchy in 1909. This change received some support from the Jews, but not the Arabs, who were unimpressed at being given only a quarter of the seats in the proposed parliament when they outnumbered the Turks in the empire as a whole. The Turks therefore suppressed any move towards Arab independence, which in turn led the Arabs to form secret societies.

A Christian Arab, Neguib Azoury, writing at this time, foresaw a serious clash between Arab nationalism and Jewish resettlement in their ancient homeland. Palestine faced a difficult situation.

Summary: the nineteenth century saw certain Jewish rabbis and writers, and Theodore Herzl in particular, call for a restoration to their biblical homeland (Zionism). The numbers moving to Palestine were small until persecution in Russia led to the first large immigration from 1881 onwards. There were early indications that there would be a conflict between Jews and Arabs in the Holy Land.

****

7. Exit the Ottomans

In 1914 the Turks joined Germany and Austria in a war against Britain, France and Russia. The situation in Palestine was put on hold, but the future of the Middle East was the subject of three high level discussions during the war.

Sharif Hussein of Mecca, a descendant of the Prophet Muhammed, was the official Protector of the Holy Places of Islam at the time. He had previously approached the British concerning their support, should he want to lead an Arab rebellion against the Turks. The British at first declined, sticking to their policy of keeping a weakened Ottoman Empire in existence as a buffer against Russia. However, when the Turks joined Germany in World War I, Britain saw that Arab support in protecting their interests in the Middle East would be an important advantage. They therefore instructed High Commissioner Henry McMahon to open a correspondence with Sharif Hussein.

In return for his support, Sharif Hussein asked for independence for all Arab provinces after the war, hoping for a unified Syria/Iraq/Arabian peninsula. His son Feisal later pointed out that Palestine was part of Greater Syria and should be included by name in his father's request. In reply, McMahon stated the areas he would exclude as not being purely Arab, including parts of Syria west of Damascus. Although he later stated that he had always intended that Palestine should be part of the excluded areas, the matter was, for some parties, not adequately clarified. The full extent of the Sharif's understanding is unknown. At the time he expressed his concerns but the matter was left for special negotiations when the Ottoman occupation ended.

Early in 1916, a Turkish-German force set out for the Yemen. Their route was via the Hejaz (Muslim Holy Places - Mecca and Medina), so the Sharif was prompted to begin the Arab revolt that the

British had hoped for. He was proclaimed King of the Arabs by his followers, but only King of the Hejaz by the British.

Even while the Hussein-McMahon correspondence was in progress, the British were holding secret negotiations with their French allies. George Picot of France and Sir Mark Sykes of Britain reached agreement early in 1916 concerning the allocation of Ottoman lands at the end of the war. The future areas of Lebanon and Syria would go to France; Iraq and Jordan to Britain (map p.49); only what is present day Saudi Arabia would be independent under the Arabs. Most of Palestine, including Jerusalem, would be under international control. This was aimed at resolving problems between Britain, France and Russia over future control of the Christian holy places.

In 1917, Sykes was sent to reassure an increasingly suspicious Sharif Hussein, without giving away full details of the 'Sykes-Picot' agreement. For his part, Hussein's Arab revolt was having an effect. By engaging significant numbers of Turkish forces in his own region, he prevented them from linking up with the Germans in East Africa, which would have closed the Red Sea to the Allies. Sharif Hussein's son Feisal led the Arab forces, with assistance from the British colonel, T.E. Lawrence (Lawrence of Arabia). Meanwhile, the British army struggled against the Turks in Palestine until General Allenby took over in 1917. He improved the situation and headed for Jerusalem, via Beersheba, just as Feisal and Lawrence captured the Red Sea port of Aqaba by means of a surprise inland attack.

A significant power change occurred in Russia late in 1917 when the Bolsheviks took control. They found documents pertaining to the Sykes-Picot agreement and immediately informed the Turks, who told Sharif Hussein. The British quickly sent McMahon's successor, Sir Reginald Wingate, to assure Sharif Hussein that the documents concerned only provisional exchanges between the Allies. The successful Arab revolt and the withdrawal of the Russians from the war changed the situation anyway, but this was not the only matter over which the Sharif would need British reassurances.

The third high level series of talks taking place during the war involving the British was with some Jewish groups. Chaim Weizmann, in particular, had been lobbying the British for a Jewish homeland in Palestine once the war was over. Some of his scientific discoveries arising from his work in Britain were of use in the war effort, so he gained a sympathetic ear. Herbert Samuel, a Member of Parliament who happened to be Jewish, suggested Britain might create a Jewish Palestine, annexed to the British Empire, and a change of government late in 1916 developed this idea. Lloyd George became Prime Minister and Balfour the Foreign Minister. Unconvinced that the Sykes-Picot agreement covered Britain's Middle East interests adequately, they pressed for a campaign to take Syria and Palestine and sent Sykes to discuss this with Weizmann. In response, the Zionists raised world-wide sympathy for a Jewish homeland in the region, thereby aiding the British plans. Withdrawal of the Russians after their 1917 Bolshevik Revolution removed another obstacle from the British plan.

In September 1917 a draft agreement between Britain and the Zionist movement was challenged by the only Jewish cabinet minister at the time, Sir Edwin Montague, Secretary of State for India. He objected to the implication that the whole of Palestine would become a Jewish national home because this would further upset anti-Semites, the Muslims of India, and even those Jews who were happy not to return to the land of their ancestors. However, with the Americans lending their support the following month, and with Allenby's army moving into Palestine, the Balfour Declaration was finalised in November 1917 (page 43).

Although the declaration deliberately avoided the word 'state', Sharif Hussein still suspected the way was clear for a Jewish state in Palestine. The British reassured him that no such state was envisaged

Balfour Declaration

Foreign Office,
November 2nd,1917.

Dear Lord Rothschild,

I have much pleasure in conveying to you, on behalf of His Majesty's Government, the following declaration of sympathy with Jewish Zionist aspirations which has been submitted to, and approved by, the Cabinet:

"His Majesty's Government view with favour the establishment in Palestine of a national home for the Jewish people, and will use their best endeavours to facilitate the achievement of this object, it being clearly understood that nothing shall be done which may prejudice the civil and religious rights of existing non-Jewish communities in Palestine, or the rights and political status enjoyed by Jews in any other country".

I should be grateful if you would bring this declaration to the knowledge of the Zionist Federation.

Yours sincerely

(signed by) Arthur James Balfour

Note: this document was a declaration of intent, as the British did not at the time it was issued possess the land concerned.

and he apparently accepted these reassurances. The Arabs in Palestine itself however, having experienced the Jewish immigration since 1881, now feared a takeover.

General Allenby's military campaign was successful. He entered Jerusalem on December 11th 1917 and declared its independence after four hundred years under the Ottomans. The following year he went on to take Damascus where Feisal's forces installed their own temporary governor, with Lawrence's support. The Turkish war effort was over.

Britain finished the war in a strong position, but recognised the higher losses suffered by its French allies. French interests were therefore put before the Arabs', who, it was claimed, were very dependent on British resources anyway. It was therefore a modified version of the Sykes-Picot agreement which was put into effect. The French were allowed to send troops to Beirut, from where they occupied the coastal area. Feisal continued to hold the Syrian interior, with the support of British officers. The British area included Palestine, with Allenby in charge. Weizmann, who had arrived early in 1918 to give advice on the Balfour Declaration, had meetings with Feisal, and they agreed to support each other at the coming Versailles Peace Conference. Feisal believed that supporting the Jewish cause would bring influential Jewish support for his own cause. At Versailles, it was decided that Turkey should forfeit all its non-Turkish areas, and that they would be reallocated at a conference the following year.

At this point, British policy was challenged, in writing, by seven influential Arabs in Cairo. Britain responded with the 'Declaration to the Seven' stating that the future government of land liberated through the action of Arab armies would be based on the principle of the 'consent of the governed'. American President Woodrow Wilson had included this idea in his 'Four Ends of Peace' which itself became part of the Covenant of the League of Nations. An Anglo-French declaration at the end of the war stated that the two countries would establish national administrations, based on the will of the local people. But how would this work out in practice?

A conference of Muslim and Christian Arabs held in Jerusalem early in 1919, called for an independent Palestine in the region of southern Syria. American interest led to the King-Crane enquiry, which found that the Arabs wanted no mandate countries, but would accept aid from America, and maybe Britain, though not France. A mandate was the power to administer, under supervision of the League of Nations, the idea being that mandated regions should become independent as soon as they were ready. The enquiry also realised that the rights of non-Jews, as per the Balfour Declaration, would place limitations on Zionist hopes. In the event, the Americans declined to act on their report when the Allies rejected it. Arab disappointment at this outcome led to the Nebi Musa riot in Jerusalem in April 1920 - the first of its kind against Zionist plans.

In the wider picture, the Arab General Syrian Congress called for the recognition of Syria, including Palestine, and Iraq, with Feisal as King of Syria. The British pressurised him into accepting the French occupation along the coast, as well as their assistance inland. The Arab Congress reacted by declaring independence for Syria/Palestine, and autonomy for Lebanon. When the people of Iraq also declared independence, with Amir Abdullah (another of Sharif Hussein's sons) as king, the British and French were put on the spot. In response they convened the Supreme Council of the League of Nations, the precursor to the United Nations, at San Remo in April 1920. The outcome was 'Partition'. Syria, apart from Palestine, was divided into Lebanon and Syria – the mandates for both going to France. Britain received the mandate for Iraq and Palestine, with responsibility for fulfilling the Balfour Declaration of 1917. This required placing Palestine under such political, administrative and economic conditions as would secure the establishment of a Jewish home. Britain would be responsible for facilitating Jewish immigration while ensuring that the rights and position of other sections of the

45

population were not prejudiced. The recently formed League of Nations (which later became the United Nations) approved the terms of this mandate in June 1922. The creation of a homeland for the Jewish people, in a land to which they had a historical connection, was thus officially recognised.

Summary: During World War I the British gained Arab military support, agreed land allocation with the French, and promised the Jewish people a homeland in part of Palestine. This led to a conflict of interests which culminated in the League of Nations allocating mandates for Lebanon and Syria to the French, and Iraq and Palestine to the British. The Arabs were left with control of Saudi Arabia.

****

8. British Mandate

Herbert Samuel was appointed as the first British High Commissioner of Palestine. On his arrival in 1920 he set up an advisory council of Christians, Jews and Muslims. His intention was to establish a partly elected legislature for the combined community. However, riots in and around Jaffa at the time were due, according to the investigative Haycroft Commission, to Arab fears of a permanent Zionist settlement, backed by the Balfour Declaration. The fact that the land registry had been re-opened, allowing legal land purchase by Jews, supported their view.

The Arabs then sent a delegation to Europe to present their case to a wider audience. They continued to press for changes in British policy and on one occasion met with Weizmann in London, but without any agreement. Meanwhile, in Jerusalem, Samuel was trying to sort out a dispute over the election for Grand Mufti. In the end he over-ruled the voting and, seeking to keep a balance between the two leading Arab families, he appointed Hajj Amin al-Husseini. This placed a strong Arab nationalist in a key position.

During negotiations with the British, the Arabs referred to the Hussein-McMahon correspondence and other assurances made during the war. The British denied that Palestine, west of the Jordan, was included in the pledge to Sharif Hussein. A British White Paper in 1922 sought to appease both parties - the Jews regarding a national home, and the Arabs regarding their not suffering from its establishment. The Balfour declaration was reaffirmed and Jewish immigration was related to employment opportunities.

Still believing that Britain was only waiting until the Jewish community became dominant before granting it independence, the Arabs rejected Samuel's legislative council by boycotting the elections. His alternative, an advisory council of eight Muslims, two Christians and two Jews, received the same treatment. They also rejected his offer of an Arab Agency to match the existing Jewish one in representing their views and needs. They believed the boycotting tactic would eventually succeed, but in fact the British gave up negotiating with them shortly after this, in 1923. Even at this early stage the British were discovering how difficult this mandate would be, given that the idea of a mandate was to bring independence to the region concerned in due course.

Further afield, Feisal briefly challenged the French, but was defeated and exiled to Britain. The British then made him King of Iraq, instead of his brother Abdullah. As the French refused to grant Abdullah a state anywhere in Syria, Britain decided to create the state of Transjordan for him. This land would have been part of Palestine east of the River Jordan, according to the San Remo conference proposal of 1920. Now Palestine would be limited to land west of that river. The whole partition was ratified by the League of Nations in 1922, thereby officially creating the new states of Iraq, Lebanon, Palestine, Syria and Transjordan. (see map page 49).

Both sides in the developing Arab – Jewish conflict proceeded to widen their support base. Firstly, an Arab Conference in 1927 extended membership to delegates from around the world, then, in 1929 the British allowed an enlarged Jewish Agency with half its membership from outside Palestine. The same year saw Arab riots relating to the right of Jews to pray at the Western Wall. This resulted in a British White Paper proposing restrictions in the two key areas of Jewish immigration and land purchases. Jewish supporters in the British government blocked these proposals, so the Arabs sought international support. A Muslim Conference produced only a limited boycott of Jewish and British goods, but Grand Mufti Hajj Amin strengthened his position when the conference sanctioned protective developments around the Western Wall.

The early 1930's saw an increase in Jewish immigration due to Hitler's rise to power in Germany, and to greater Jewish confidence in Palestine as trade developed.

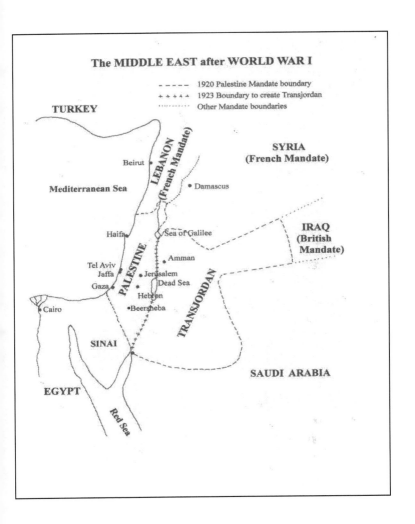

The MIDDLE EAST after WORLD WAR I

- - - - - 1920 Palestine Mandate boundary
＋＋＋＋＋ 1923 Boundary to create Transjordan
··········· Other Mandate boundaries

TURKEY

LEBANON
(French Mandate)

SYRIA
(French Mandate)

Beirut

Mediterranean Sea

• Damascus

Haifa

Sea of Galilee

IRAQ
(British
Mandate)

PALESTINE

• Amman

Tel Aviv
Jaffa
Gaza

• Jerusalem
Dead Sea
Hebron
•Beersheba

TRANSJORDAN

• Cairo

SINAI

SAUDI ARABIA

EGYPT

Red Sea

Note: originally the Sykes-Picot talks gave Britain the
mandate for Jordan, which covered Palestine and Transjordan
on the map above. When Abdullah lost out to Feisal as King of
Iraq, the British compensated by giving him the land 'across
the Jordan' or Transjordan. This left the area indicated on the
map above as Palestine to the British Mandate.

A right-wing Zionist movement led by Jabotinsky began pushing for as many Jews as possible to enter Palestine, legally or otherwise. By 1935 the Arabs were again asking for Jewish land purchases and immigration to be cut, and for democratic rule to be introduced. The British suggested a legislative council of fourteen Arabs, eight Jews and six British. Most Arabs rejected it because the proportion did not match their population, while at the same time the Jews felt it would hand development of the land over to the Arabs.

In 1936 Arab fears of Jewish dominance and the apparent inability of the British to respond, resulted in an Arab rebellion against the Mandate. They set up an Arab Higher Committee (AHC), with Hajj Amin as leader. There was a six months strike and the beginnings of an Arab fighting force. While the British military dealt with the violence, the politicians sent in another commission.

The Peel Commission of 1937 reported that the two key factors behind the rebellion were the Arab fear that a Jewish national homeland was being established, while at the same time they were being refused their own national independence. Peel then came up with a new idea, namely partition into Jewish and Arab states within the land of Palestine. Jerusalem and the key port of Haifa would remain under British control, and Jewish immigration would be limited to 12,000 a year. The Arab state would combine with Transjordan, which was part of the original British mandate before they created a state for Abdullah.

In considering Peel's plan, the Jews appreciated the fact that a 'state' was now being proposed. The Zionist Congress therefore voted in favour, led by Weizmann and Ben Gurion, though the more right-wing Jabotinsky opposed it. King Abdullah, who had been making steady progress in Transjordan with British support, liked the plan, thinking that the Zionist potential might lead to the Arabs living in Palestine wanting to be part of his kingdom. The Arabs themselves boycotted participation in the Peel Commission until Arab leaders in surrounding countries persuaded them otherwise. They then rejected the partition plan and stepped up their rebellion. In response, the British deported all the AHC members except Hajj Amin, who escaped and ended up in Baghdad. The League of Nations authorised further work on the partition idea, but conferences, which included Arabs from surrounding countries, failed to make any real progress. The rebellion faded away early in 1939 when the British sent in more troops.

The Mandate had seen several attempts by the Arabs to bring the British round to their way of thinking. However, when the British came up with proposals arising from their commissions, the local Arab response tended to be negative, often against the advice of the wider Arab world. Under Hajj Amin in particular, they appeared unwilling to compromise. Meanwhile, the Jews had established their own assembly, tax system, trade union, university and secret army. Their land holdings had doubled and their settlements numbered around two hundred. Their more extreme wing, under Jabotinsky, advocated what became known as the 'iron wall' of military defence against the Arabs. The comparatively moderate Social Zionists, under Ben Gurion, preferred to rely on support from major powers and thus supported Britain's partition plan.

The British assumed the Jews would side with them against Hitler in the approaching World War II, but they also wanted Arab support. Aware that Hajj Amin had entered into talks with Germany, they decided to meet the Arab representatives in London, on condition that Hajj Amin would not be present. The resulting British White Paper limited Jewish immigration to 75,000 over the next five years with any increase subject to Arab approval. An Arab state within ten years was also intended. The Arabs rejected these proposals because they thought the immigration restrictions were inadequate. Furthermore, they did not trust the British to carry them through, based on their experiences in World War I in general, and the McMahon-Hussein correspondence in particular. However, they decided that they could not rely on Germany either. The Jews thought the proposals fell so far short of Balfour that they pushed on towards establishing their own state regardless. Their approach was summarised by Ben Gurion: 'We will fight with the British against Hitler as if there were no White Paper; we will fight the White Paper as if there were no war.' Officially there was a truce between Arabs, Jews and the British during the war, but the Jews did set up resistance groups such as the Palmach force to defend themselves against the Arabs and, if necessary, the Germans. Some Palestinians, both Arabs and Jews fought with the Allies against Germany. The numbers quoted vary, but are usually higher for the Jewish contribution. A Jewish brigade, formed late in the war, adopted the Star of David as its emblem, which later became the national flag.

Many Jews fled the Nazi persecution, and there were efforts to get some of them into Palestine, despite a British blockade. Thousands were turned away and interned in Cyprus. The German threat in the Middle East itself subsided when the British, under Field Marshal Montgomery, defeated them in North Africa, The Jewish underground, Menachem Begin's Irgun, then revolted in Palestine. They were angry about the British blockade tactics, especially in light of emerging information about the Holocaust. They also suspected the British would eventually abandon the Jewish population of Palestine. After a while, Ben Gurions's Haganah began working with the Irgun, and the more extremist Stern Gang, against the British. At this stage some British officers, including John Bagot Glubb, known as 'Glubb Pasha', who had trained the Transjordanian Arab forces, advised partition overseen by troops. Lord Moyne, British Minister of State in Cairo, was killed by the Stern Gang before he could respond to this idea.

During the war Ben Gurion and Weizmann attended an American Zionist meeting which produced the Biltmore Plan. This claimed the whole of Palestine for the Jewish people as they anticipated vast numbers of refugees when the war ended. When the scale of the Holocaust became apparent, this claim received a lot of international support. The Zionists generally moved towards the Americans as the emerging power of the future, especially with its interest in Middle-Eastern oil. The British, though victors in the region, were on the decline, exhausted by their war effort.

Summary: British attempts to establish a legislature in Palestine acceptable to all parties were unsuccessful. Instead, the idea of dividing the land into Jewish and Arab states was proposed. The Second World War put matters on hold but it did produce large numbers of Jewish refugees from Europe who wanted to settle in Palestine.

****

9. Exit the British

When the World War II ended in 1945, American President Truman pressed Britain to allow 100,000 Jewish refugees into Palestine. British Foreign Secretary Bevan responded with an Anglo-American Commission of Enquiry which reported in April 1946. It recommended the continuation of the Mandate without restrictions on land sales or Jewish immigration, but with the disarming of the Jewish underground. The British deemed such a plan to be unworkable but allowed some discussions on Arab and Jewish autonomy. They continued to restrict Jewish immigration, incurring a strong response from the underground forces; for example, the bombing of British offices in the King David Hotel Jerusalem, which killed ninety-one people. For its part, the recently formed Arab League was stressing the Arab character of Palestine.

Britain was caught between its interests in the Arab countries and the pressure from America, on which it was financially dependent due to the cost of the war effort. After one final attempt at Arab-Jewish agreement, the British handed the problem over to the United Nations early in 1947, in the hope that the UN could resolve a situation which Britain had struggled with for nearly thirty years.

The UN set up UNSCOP – United Nations Special Commission on Palestine, whose members came from: Australia, Canada, Czechoslovakia, Guatemala, Netherlands, Peru, Sweden, Uruguay, India, Iran and Yugoslavia. It began work in May 1947 and soon found that unanimous agreement was unlikely. A minority report from India, Iran and Yugoslavia, preferred a federal state with Jerusalem as its capital. Australia abstained. The other seven nations produced a majority report which took the partition idea a step further by recommending that there should be separate Arab and Jewish states.

The Arab Higher Committee boycotted UNSCOP, objecting to its suggestion that Palestine was the answer to the European Jewish refugee problem, and to the way it was allocating agricultural land. As with other commissions, they felt it ignored the rights of Arabs as the majority of the indigenous population. The Arab League rejected the report and prepared to defend its borders with Palestine, should a Jewish state pose a threat to them. Another UN committee, with Jewish and Palestinian representatives, discussed the situation in the autumn of 1947. The Arab delegation rejected partition and renewed its demands for independence.

A significant move came late in November when UN resolution 181 ratified the plan for partition into Arab and Jewish states, but with Jerusalem under international control. The voting was thirty-three to thirteen with ten abstentions, including Britain. America and Russia put their considerable influence behind the resolution. The Zionist executive accepted it but the Arabs (AHC) went to the International Court of Justice, challenging the UN for partitioning a country against the wishes of its majority. They narrowly lost their appeal.

The Mandate was set to end in May 1948, but the British declined full co-operation with the UN body overseeing the transition period because they felt the plan was not acceptable to both Arabs and Jews. Instead, they began handing over to whichever party, Arabs or Jews, was better placed to control a given town or locality. This resulted in a very messy and confusing situation. There were many local struggles for power which led, in effect, to civil war. This outcome worried the Americans who objected to partition by force, and called for a truce. The Zionists responded by stepping up their efforts to establish a state, implementing what they called 'Plan D', aimed at securing the land allocated to the Jewish state by UN resolution 181. They met with some opposition from the Arab Liberation Army but gained control of major towns and much of Jerusalem. The intensity of the conflict was evidenced by the Jewish attack on the village of

55

Deir Yassin, followed a few days later by an Arab attack on a medical convoy in Jerusalem. As in many incidents to come, claims regarding the number of casualties varied according to which side's version you listened to. However, casualties there certainly were, many of them civilian.

Summary: After the end of World War II the British tried once again to resolve the problem of how Palestine should be ruled before handing the whole situation over to the United Nations. UN resolution 181 decreed partition into Arab and Jewish states, to take effect in May 1948. The British failed to manage a smooth transition and violence ensued.

****

10. A New State and Matters Arising

However it drew the borders, the UN partition plan for Palestine could not avoid mixing Arabs and Jews. It gave the Jewish state similar numbers of Arabs and Jews, while the Arab state had a large majority of its own people. When Ben Gurion declared the Jewish State of Israel on May 15th 1948, the Americans backed him because they saw Israel as a bastion of democracy in the Middle East. The Russians backed him because they wanted the British out of the area, and because they believed the Jewish state would become socialist due to the strong influence of the Social Zionists, such as Ben Gurion.

The Arab countries responded by immediately invading from all sides and Israel's War of Independence began. The Arab forces started well, but although they represented millions of Arabs against approximately 600,000 Jews, their regular armies were not sufficiently united to overcome a people fighting for its survival. King Abdullah of Transjordan had even been in secret talks with the Jewish leadership, with an eye to taking the Arab part of Palestine under his own wing.

UN mediator Bernadotte arranged cease-fires but made no progress with his settlement proposals. He was then assassinated by the Jewish Stern Gang, who viewed him as an agent of the British. After this, the Stern Gang and the Irgun were absorbed by the Haganah, which itself had been renamed the Israel Defence Force (IDF). The IDF fared better after the initial truce, its rate of mobilisation outstripping that of the Arab armies. They freed up the road to Jerusalem, which had been under siege, but the Arab Legion held on to the Old City. The Israelis left the West Bank (of the River Jordan) alone, but took the Negev from the Egyptian army.

The fighting ended in January 1949, after which another UN mediator arranged a series of armistices between the two sides. The outcome of the war for the Jews was the establishment of the State of

Israel, which was admitted to the UN in May 1949. The Arabs were left with less land than the partition plan would have given them, (see map page 61), so they refer to this war as 'Al-Nakba' – the Great Catastrophe.

The UN was unable to follow up the armistices with any peace treaties, mainly because of the number of Arab refugees displaced by the war. This number varies according whether it dates from November 1947 or later, and which source you refer to, but it amounted to hundreds of thousands rather than tens of thousands. Some left their homes to avoid the war; some left 'temporarily' in response to the advice of invading Arab armies, expecting to return after their victory; and some were removed by the IDF. Again, the numbers applied to each of these reasons vary according to source of information. Whatever the total number may have been, the Arabs insisted on the right of return for these refugees, while Israel would only discuss the matter as part of an overall peace agreement. The Arab League blamed Israel for the refugee problem, and pushed the UN to demand either a return to their original homes, or compensation from Israel for loss of property. Israel handed responsibility for the refugees to the Arabs because they had rejected the UN resolution 181 on Palestine and then started the war.

In January 1949 Ben Gurion became Prime Minister of Israel and took the view that the present situation would eventually be accepted without his having to concede refugee rights and land in return for peace. The Arabs continued to insist on the refugee problem being resolved before entering any peace treaty, although King Abdullah did accommodate a significant number of refugees inside Jordan. What remained of Arab Palestine, including East Jerusalem and its Old City, came under his rule and was referred to as the 'West Bank' (West of the River Jordan).

There were also Jewish refugees in the aftermath of the 1948 war. Large numbers of Jews were compelled to leave the surrounding Arab countries, many of them arriving in Israel. Israel treated the ceasefire lines as international boundaries within which people could be settled. The Arabs, on the other hand, there being no peace treaties, assumed they were still in a state of war, and believed that Israel could not settle in these areas. The UN's Palestine Conciliation Commission was the first attempt to resolve this issue. It failed.

The UN partition plan had designated Jerusalem for international control, but the war had left it divided into East and West along the Israeli-Jordanian cease-fire line. The Jewish state wanted the city as its capital because of its historical and religious importance. It was opposed by three groups of countries pushing for its internationalisation: the Muslim states who generally supported the Arab cause and were concerned about their holy sites on the Temple Mount; the Roman Catholic states, led by the Vatican, who were concerned about the Christian holy sites; and the Russian bloc, which was also concerned about the Christian holy sites, but on behalf of the Eastern Orthodox church.

In December 1949, Ben Gurion said that while UN supervision over the holy sites was acceptable, foreign rule over Jerusalem itself was not. The UN responded with a well supported resolution to place the city under its control, to which Israel replied by stating that they would move their Knesset (parliament) from Tel Aviv to Jerusalem. This was done by January 1st 1950 and followed up with a proclamation that Jerusalem was the eternal capital of the Jewish state. Ben Gurion argued that conceding the whole city to the UN would lead to demands regarding holy sites elsewhere in the country, followed by pressure to take back refugees. He managed to defy the UN resolution, but the status of Jerusalem became an ongoing issue and remains so today.

King Abdullah was as keen to hold on to his part of the city as the Israelis were to hold on to theirs, so when the Knesset moved to Jerusalem, he responded by granting Jordanian citizenship to the Arab inhabitants of East Jerusalem, as well as to those in the West Bank (Judea and Samaria). His armistice agreement with Israel allowed Jewish access to the Western Wall, but this did not actually happen, and a lot of Jewish property in the Old City was damaged. Israel did continue talks with King Abdullah, however, until he was killed by a Muslim extremist when visiting the Old City in July 1951.

Arab refugees, Jewish settlements and the status of Jerusalem became major long-term issues in the Holy Land. To these three can be added the issue of water resources. At this stage it was water rights in the north which were affecting the peace talks with Syria. As the population grew, so the demand for water would become more serious and potentially divisive.

The Law of Return passed by the Knesset in 1950 encouraged a big increase in Jewish immigration from countries over and above those Arab countries from which many Jews were already fleeing. There were also approximately 150,000 Arabs who found themselves living in the new state of Israel, with West Jerusalem as its capital. The Knesset's Nationality Law gave equal rights to all citizens, including these 'Israeli Arabs'. How this would work out in practice remained to be seen.

It is important to point out here that if the Arabs who found themselves within the new State of Israel are referred to as Israeli Arabs, then the Arabs in the rest of the territory to which the UN had addressed its partition plan could from now on be referred to as Palestinian Arabs. The UN sought to help the Palestinian Arab refugees in the surrounding countries, by setting up UNRWA – The United Nations Relief and Works Agency. Many of these Palestinian Arabs attempted to slip back to their homes in what was now Israel, in order to be re-united with their families, thus creating an infiltration situation along the borders. They also, in effect, became Israeli Arabs by crossing the border.

A new development in the early 1950's was Gamal Nasser's rise to power in Egypt. Israel saw a threat in this, especially as Nassar had access to Russian arms. The Americans had pulled out of supplying

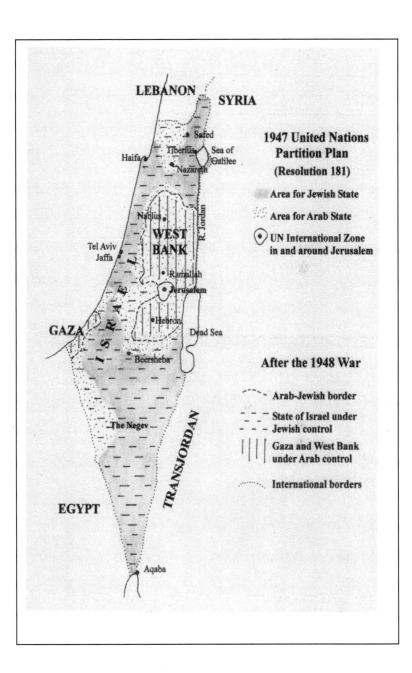

1947 United Nations
Partition Plan
(Resolution 181)

Area for Jewish State

Area for Arab State

UN International Zone
in and around Jerusalem

After the 1948 War

Arab-Jewish border

State of Israel under
Jewish control

Gaza and West Bank
under Arab control

International borders

61

arms to Israel after its excessive retaliation against Syria in a dispute over fishing rights in Galilee. However, because of Nasser's aid to Algerian independence fighters, France was willing to arm Israel. Significantly, they also agreed to supply a nuclear power plant (at Dimona) as part of the 'Challe Plan', which involved Britain, to deal with Nasser after he had nationalised the Suez Canal in July 1956.

The Challe Plan was put into effect in October 1956, when the IDF parachuted troops into the Mitla Pass, 30 miles east of Suez. They reached the canal the next day, at which point the British and French issued a pre-arranged ultimatum requiring both sides to withdraw ten miles. As anticipated, the Egyptians refused, giving the Allies an excuse to bomb their airfields. Nasser quickly withdrew to cut his losses and the IDF took the whole of Sinai within a few days. However, this 'set-up' was strongly challenged by America and Russia, bringing a humiliating end to the British and French action, and the withdrawal of the IDF from Sinai. A UN force was put in place rather than leaving a vacuum around the canal.

Because of its co-operation with Britain and France over Suez, Israel came to seen by the Arabs as a bridgehead for western imperialism into the Arab world. However, America continued to deny arms support to Israel, being more interested in maintaining stability in the region, with oil interests in mind. Other NATO, (North Atlantic Treaty Organisation) countries also declined to help. Syria and Egypt then formed their short-lived United Arab Republic (UAR) in 1958, which threatened to encircle Israel, adding urgency to its need for allies. Looking elsewhere, Israel found allies in: Iran, which was then on poor terms with its Arab neighbours; Turkey, which was pro-Western and allied to America; and Ethiopia, which was having problems with Egypt over water sources. Relations with a number of other African countries were developed at this time.

The Suez crisis had also affected the Arab world. In 1958 civil war broke out in Lebanon between President Chamoun's mainly Christian, pro-Western regime, and the Muslim Socialist Nationalist

Front, which wanted to join the United Arab Republic. In the same year, a military coup in Iraq (which had been backing Chamoun) put Abdul Qasim, of the Free Officers Group, in power. Meanwhile in Jordan, King Hussein only survived with British support. These developments further reflected the Arab intention to encircle Israel. In response, Israel made some progress when the nuclear reactor from France was upgraded, placing a nuclear deterrent within reach. Also, John F Kennedy became American President and leaned more towards Israel, eventually supplying the country with missiles.

With water resources in mind, Israel had moved quickly to complete its project to pipe water from the Sea of Galilee, all the way to the Negev by 1964. One of the sea's sources came from Syria, another from Lebanon. This caused the Arab League members to take action against what they saw as the diversion of some of 'their' water. In order to present this, and the whole Palestinian Arab cause, to the wider world, the Palestine Liberation Organisation (PLO) was established in 1964, with Ahmed Sukhari as chairman. There was a national assembly in East Jerusalem and representatives from around the world. Their charter called for the liquidation of Israel and the return of Arab refugees. They established the Palestinian Liberation Army (PLA), which tried to divert the Sea of Galilee's sources in Syria and Lebanon, but they were prevented from achieving this aim by the IDF.

Guerrilla attacks continued, however, especially by Fatah – a group which had been formed by Yasser Arafat a few years earlier. Fearing the PLA would fall under the control of the Arab regimes, he requested that Fatah operate in its own right as a secret unit. The PLO refused, for fear of damaging its relations with Arab governments, but some Fatah fighters still carried out independent assaults against Israel, thereby maintaining at least some evidence of an ongoing armed struggle. Guerilla operations received a boost when radical Ba'athists took power in Syria in 1966. King Hussein of Jordan, though, was far less supportive of guerrilla action and was therefore shocked by an IDF reprisal against one of his villages, Samu, which killed several of his soldiers. Having thus damaged relations with the more moderate Jordan, Israel then escalated the fight with Syria. A dispute over the De-Militarised Zone in the Golan Heights ended with Israeli jets downing six Syrian MiGs, and Damascus expecting a full-scale attack. Russia backed Syria and encouraged Nasser to act. He responded by sending troops into Sinai, and closing Israeli shipping access through the Persian Gulf. When King Hussein joined the surge of Arab nationalism by signing a defence pact with Syria, the scene was set for another war.

Summary: Israel declared its independence in May 1948 and survived a war with the surrounding Arab nations, ending up with more land than the UN resolution had allocated. Key issues arising from the war were the status of Jerusalem, Arab refugees, Jewish settlers and water resources.

Arabs resident within the borders of the new State of Israel were referred to as Israeli Arabs, so the term Palestinian Arabs came to refer to those outside the borders. These Palestinian Arabs established a liberation organisation (the PLO) to maintain the fight against the State of Israel.

****

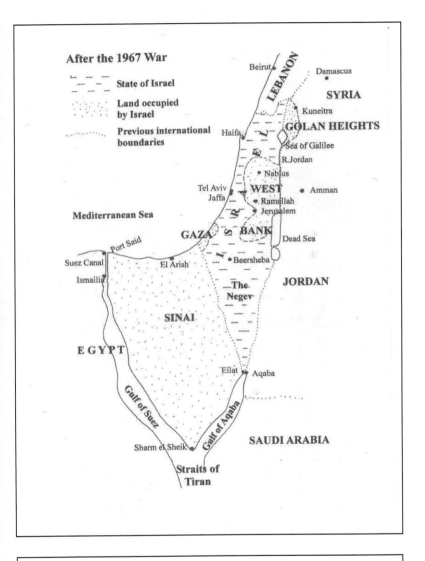

After the 1967 War

State of Israel

Land occupied by Israel

Previous international boundaries

Beirut

Damascus

LEBANON

SYRIA

Kuneitra

GOLAN HEIGHTS

Haifa

Sea of Galilee

R. Jordan

Nablus

Tel Aviv

Jaffa

WEST

Amman

Ramallah

Jerusalem

Mediterranean Sea

GAZA

BANK

Dead Sea

Port Said

ISRAEL

Suez Canal

El Arish

Beersheba

Ismailia

The Negev

JORDAN

SINAI

EGYPT

Eilat

Aqaba

Gulf of Suez

Gulf of Aqaba

Sharm el Sheik

SAUDI ARABIA

Straits of Tiran

As a result of this war, Israel acquired the Sinai, the Gaza Strip, the West Bank (including East Jerusalem) and the Golan Heights – all referred to as 'occupied territory' by the Palestinian Arabs, and indeed, by the UN. Sinai would be returned to Egypt in 1981, and the Gaza Strip handed over to the Palestinian Authority in 2005. The other areas remain under dispute.

11. More Wars

In response to Arab manoeuvres, Israel formed a national unity government at the beginning of June 1967 and, after receiving a green light from America, decided to go to war. Nasser held back from striking first for fear that his Russian arms suppliers would prefer him not to be seen as the aggressor. This gave Israel the initiative, which they took by destroying the Egyptian air force on the ground. Aircraft from Iraq, Jordan and Syria then attacked but were decisively beaten. IDF forces quickly defeated the Egyptians in Sinai and established themselves on the east bank of the Suez Canal.

Israel had asked King Hussein to keep out of the conflict. But, encouraged by (false) reports of Egyptian successes, and his own desire to take the whole of Jerusalem, he declined. His forces began shelling West Jerusalem, leading the Israeli government to capture East Jerusalem in order to stop him. They first encircled it and then, under General Moshe Dayan's orders, when he heard the UN was calling for a cease-fire, moved in. The next day saw a divided Jerusalem re-united and the Temple Mount under Jewish control. The Jordanians retreated across the Jordan, allowing the IDF to invade the West Bank. Wary that Russia might intervene to support Syria, Jewish settlers put pressure on their government to take the Golan Heights. Dayan held off until he intercepted a message from Nasser to the Syrian president, urging him to call for a cease-fire. The IDF then went ahead, capturing the Golan Heights before a UN cease-fire took effect the following day.

What became known as 'The Six Day War' lasted from, June 5th – 10th 1967. Israel emerged as the dominant military force and gained large areas of land, including all of East Jerusalem. Their success brought with it the responsibility for 750,000 Palestinian Arabs and the third holiest site of Islam. Approximately 300,000 Arabs had fled to Jordan from the West Bank and around 100,000 from the Golan into Syria, thereby significantly increasing the refugee problem. The Jewish people on the other hand now occupied the whole of what they recognised as their capital city after an absence of two thousand years.

The UN response was resolution 242, passed in November 1967. It called for the Arab states to recognise Israel's right to exist, in return for Israel's withdrawal from the territories gained as a result of the war. It also called for freedom of navigation through the Suez Canal and Persian Gulf, and a just settlement of the refugee problem.

Israel's government had actually annexed East Jerusalem before resolution 242 arrived, thus making clear its claim to sovereignty over this part of its ancient homeland. But Israel had also offered the return of some land for peace with Egypt and Syria at that time. For the now occupied West Bank of the River Jordan, their Allon Plan proposed an Israeli security zone along the Jordan valley. It excluded Jericho, which would be connected to Jordan by a narrow corridor of land.

Arab leaders had met in Khartoum at the end of August 1967 and agreed a policy toward Israel of 'no recognition, no negotiation, no peace'. The National Palestinian Covenant of 1968 envisaged the total liberation of Palestine and the removal of Israel. At that time Palestinians were defined as 'Arab citizens living in Palestine up to 1947', and then anyone born of a Palestinian father after that date. Even Jews living permanently in Palestine prior to the Zionist invasion qualified as Palestinian. Note that this definition would include Israeli Arabs because it uses the date 1947, i.e. before the new State of Israel came into existence.

Fatah, under Arafat, continued its armed struggle. Guerilla bases were set up in Jordan from where they made raids into Israel. An IDF attempt to remove one of these bases resulted in defeat at Karameh, early in 1968, giving much encouragement to the Palestinian fighters. Later that year came the first plane hijacking by Palestinians, introducing an element of international terrorism to the conflict.

In September 1970, Palestinian guerrillas hijacked three western airliners and landed them in Jordan. Seriously disturbed by this action, King Hussein responded by removing the PLO infrastructure from his country and successfully repulsing a Syrian attempt to invade. This episode became known as 'Black September'. The PLO leadership fled to Lebanon.

In Egypt, Nasser's successor Anwar Sadat tried for an interim settlement with Israel, but Israel's premier, Golda Meir, preferred to maintain the status quo. This led to a stalemate, despite superpower involvement. Sadat then expelled thousands of Russian advisors in 1972 and the following year made a final effort to reach a political settlement. In Israel, however, confidence was high, and the only settlement Dayan was calling for was that of Jews into the occupied territories. A vision of a 'Greater Israel' had come out of the 1967 war, one which meant occupying more of the land from its biblical days. This would include, for example, Judea, because of its relation to the tribe of Judah and its line of kings.

Israel was taken by surprise by the next Arab offensive. In October 1973 a combined Egyptian-Syrian force attacked on the Jewish feast of Yom Kippur, hence the name 'Yom Kippur War' although it was also during the Muslim fast of Ramadan so the Arabs refer to it as 'The Ramadan War'. The Egyptians established themselves east of the Suez Canal, while the Syrians invaded the Golan and were poised to enter Galilee. Jordan, Iraq and some other Arab states contributed forces. The Saudis led an oil boycott against countries supporting Israel – such was the extent of oil production in the Middle East by then.

America and Russia sent arms to Israel and Egypt respectively. The IDF hit back, first re-capturing the Golan, then making the necessary breakthrough in Sinai. As they moved on towards Cairo and Damascus, the two super-powers threatened to enter the battlefield. In the event, they sponsored a cease-fire which ended hostilities under UN resolution 338 on October 22nd 1973. Through his 'shuttle diplomacy', America's Henry Kissinger achieved disengagement agreements between the major combatants by the spring of 1974.

Golda Meir and Moshe Dayan took most of the blame for Israel's complacency. Yitzhak Rabin replaced Golda Meir, but having a government with a tiny majority, he could make little progress with the Arab states. Then in April 1975 the Lebanese civil war broke out between the conservative Maronite Christian Phalangists and the radical Sunni Muslims, the latter allied with the PLO. Israel came to an arrangement with Syria regarding support for the Phalangists, which allowed large numbers of Syrian troops into central and northern Lebanon. The PLO, since being thrown out of Jordan (Black September) for trying to establish a state within a state there, had been trying to do the same in South Lebanon. They managed to acquire recognition from several countries and Arafat was invited to speak at the UN. When Jimmy Carter became the American President in 1977, he expressed support for the creation of a 'Palestinian homeland'.

Summary: A war lasting six days in 1967 left Israel with additional areas of land including all of East Jerusalem. UN resolution 242 called for Israel to withdraw from these areas in return for Arab recognition of its right to exist. There was no progress through negotiation and Palestinian guerrilla action continued, though its operational base had to be moved from Jordan to South Lebanon. Israel survived another war with the surrounding Arab countries in 1973

****

12. Peace Talks

The years following the 1973 war saw the decline of the Israeli Labour party, such that it lost a general election for the first time, in 1977. Menachem Begin's right-wing Nationalist Likud party gained power. It viewed the West Bank as part of 'Greater Israel', and began building settlements there. President Carter disapproved but American mediation between Israel and Egypt continued because both sides showed some interest in making peace - Egypt for economic reasons, Israel for security.

After a series of exploratory meetings and various setbacks, Egypt's President Sadat made a historic visit to Israel in November 1978. He brought with him the slogan, 'No more war', and his speech to the Knesset was well received by many around the world. The two leaders privately agreed in principle to peace for the return of occupied land to Egypt. The other Arab states would have nothing to do with Sadat's initiative and declared an economic and diplomatic boycott of Egypt. They were against Egypt making a separate peace treaty, especially if it failed to deliver Palestinian autonomy. However, President Carter persevered and in September 1978 brought the two sides together for a summit at Camp David in America. Israeli settlements in Sinai and the future of Jerusalem emerged as two key problems. Carter narrowly managed to resolve the differences, resulting in a framework for peace in the Middle East, and a peace treaty between Egypt and Israel. UN resolution 242 was to be the agreed basis, thereby including the Palestinian issue.

Six months later the treaty was completed and the Nobel Peace Prize was awarded to Sadat and Begin. Israel would withdraw from Sinai in stages, removing existing settlements in the process, and full diplomatic relations would be established. Other aspects covered security and freedom of navigation. Israel's oil supply was guaranteed, as was American support for the region if required. Sadat and Begin were committed to start discussing Palestinian autonomy within a month of the treaty being ratified. Was peace coming to the Holy Land at last?

The treaty was ratified in March 1979, at which point Egypt was expelled from the Arab League. But there had been another major development two months earlier. An Islamic revolution in Iran removed the Shah and saw the exiled Ayatollah Khomeini return to lead the new government. He set about establishing a state that would apply Islamic (Shariah) law to its own people and to the situation in surrounding countries. Jerusalem's position as the third holiest city in Islam therefore gained more importance, as did the desire to reclaim lands once ruled by Islam, including Israel. This major change in Iran was a factor in Israel's formally annexing East Jerusalem, which it had captured during the Six Day War of 1967 and, in the following year, 1980, declaring Jerusalem as its capital city. The international response was measured by the fact that very few embassies were moved from Tel Aviv to Jerusalem. However, before Iran could become too involved in the Palestinian situation, it was diverted by war with Iraq, initiated by that country's president, Saddam Hussein.

Meanwhile Sadat encouraged the PLO to talk with Israel. With its southern border secured by the treaty with Egypt, and Jordan on its eastern flank having expelled the PLO, Israel was concentrating on its northern borders. It was concerned about the PLO bases in Southern Lebanon, as well as Iraq. Fearing that Saddam Hussein might acquire nuclear weapons, they bombed his reactor at Osirak, near Baghdad, in June 1981. The Israeli government survived the resulting international condemnation.

The peace process suffered a setback when Sadat was assassinated by Islamic extremists in October 1981. He was succeeded by Hosni Mubarak. Israel did complete its withdrawal from Sinai in March 1982, but formally annexed the Golan Heights at the same time – bringing international protests. In June the shooting of the Israeli ambassador in London, by the Abu Nidal terrorist group, provided

Israel with a reason to launch their campaign to remove the PLO from South Lebanon.

Operation 'Peace for Galilee' June 1982, saw the IDF move into Southern Lebanon as far as Beirut, where they linked up with the Christian Phalangists. The Americans intervened and arranged for Arafat and the PLO to leave Beirut for Tunis. The Israelis had therefore achieved their aim of removing the PLO, but they failed to prevent the Phalangists from killing over 300 people in the Sabra and Shatila refugee camps during a search for terrorists. International condemnation of this massacre led to an Israeli commission of enquiry, which in turn led to the removal of defence minister Ariel Sharon and several senior officers.

Israel's opportunity to establish a friendly neighbour on its northern border had gone. It now faced attacks from the newly formed Iranian-backed Shi'ite Hezbollah (Party of God) instead. International credit Israel had gained from the Egyptian peace treaty was damaged by its operation into Lebanon. So, Begin resigned and was replaced by Yitshak Shamir, who had to alternate premiership with Labour's Shimon Peres due to a very close election outcome. Peres withdrew the IDF from Lebanon, and improved relations with Egypt by allowing a dispute over Taba, near Eilat, to go to arbitration. He also met with the King of Jordan to prepare the way for peace negotiations.

Summary: American sponsored negotiations between Egypt and Israel led to a peace treaty in 1979. With Egyptian and Jordanian borders comparatively secure, Israel addressed its northern border. A military operation into Southern Lebanon resulted in the PLO's removal to Tunis, but a loss of international credit due to a refugee camp massacre by Israel's Lebanese allies. The PLO was replaced in South Lebanon by Hezbollah guerrillas, supported by Iran after its Islamic revolution.

****

13. Intifada

With the PLO exiled in Tunis, the Palestinians were frustrated by the lack of interest in their plight from Arab states, as well as by an increasing number of Jewish settlements in the West Bank. Their economy was weak, and many of them had to cross daily into Israel to work. By now a whole generation (since 1967) had grown up in the refugee camps.

The outcome was a popular uprising known as an 'Intifada' - from the Arabic word meaning 'to shake off'. This first one was triggered by a traffic incident in a Gaza refugee camp in December 1987. Demonstrations spread across the region with stone-throwing, tyre-burning, strikes, and the raising of the Palestinian flag. Use of arms was the exception rather than the rule, the Palestinian Arabs not being officially allowed guns by the Israelis at this time, so it became known also as the 'Stone Intifada'. The PLO did not start it, but a control group called the National Unified Command did emerge. Israel responded with arrests, deportation, curfews and varying degrees of crowd control, including the use of tear gas and rubber bullets. The uprising affected Israel's morale and international standing. Its army, the IDF, found dealing with a whole population a very different matter to fighting another army.

The persistence of the Intifada gave the PLO and Arafat greater status, which in turn led King Hussein to abandon his hopes of taking responsibility for the West Bank as part of Jordan. This left the Arabs in the West Bank stateless, in effect, so the PLO then declared its intention to establish an independent Palestinian state, with (East) Jerusalem as its capital and Arafat as president. Its National Council declared full recognition of UN Resolutions 242 and 338, thereby indicating its acceptance of Israel's right to exist. It also renounced terrorism (see upper page 74).

From the Palestinian Declaration of Independence: November 1988.

"…The Palestinian National Council, in the name of God, and in the name of the Palestinian people, hereby proclaims the establishment of the State of Palestine on our Palestinian territory with its capital Jerusalem…"

"…The State of Palestine herewith declares that it believes in the settlement of regional and international disputes by peaceful means, in accordance with the UN charter and resolutions. Without prejudice to its natural right to defend its territorial integrity and independence, it therefore rejects the threat or use of force, violence and terrorism against its territorial integrity or political independence, as it also rejects their use against the territorial integrity of other states…"

From the Hamas Charter 1988.

"Hamas regards Nationalism as part and parcel of the religious faith. Nothing is loftier or deeper in Nationalism than waging Jihad against the enemy and confronting him when he sets foot on the land of the Muslims. And this becomes an individual duty binding on every Muslim man and woman:…"

(from Article 12)

"When our enemies usurp some Islamic lands, Jihad becomes the duty binding on all Muslims. In order to face the usurpation of Palestine by the Jews, we have no escape from raising the banner of Jihad…"

(from Article 15)

It seemed the PLO was changing from being a liberation movement into an independence movement. This challenged America to become involved in negotiations again, which it did until continued terrorist attacks against Israelis led to its withdrawal, citing PLO violation of their renunciation of terrorism.

The Intifada divided Israelis into those who saw the need to find a political solution to the Palestinian problem along the lines of a two state system, and those who demanded a hard-line approach with no land concessions. Prime Minister Shamir took the latter course. The Intifada therefore continued, but under increasing influence from Islamic fundamentalists. Hamas, related to Egypt's Muslim Brotherhood, only more willing to fight, had been founded by a small group of men, including Sheikh Ahmed Yassin, in 1986. It now came out and rejected the two-state solution, having no intention of recognising Israel. For Hamas it was a matter of reclaiming land once previously possessed by Islam, (see lower page 74 for an example). Another Islamic fundamentalist group around at this time was Islamic Jihad, which originated in the late 1970s. They took the line that Palestine had suffered from corrupt, non-Islamic leadership and that the Arab nationalist movements were unduly affected by Western influences. Arafat's response was to revert back to calling for total liberation. He also looked to Iraq's Saddam Hussein for support.

The Iraq-Iran war had ended in stalemate in 1988 and Saddam was now turning his attention elsewhere. In August 1990 he invaded Kuwait, causing Israel to put their air force on alert for fear of his weapons of mass destruction. Saddam then offered to withdraw from Kuwait if Israel withdrew from occupied Arab territory. Israel and America rejected Saddam's attempt to connect the Gulf and Palestinian situations, so the PLO sided with Iraq. In October 1990 a group of Jewish Temple Mount loyalists, who believe a third Temple should be built on that site, held prayers there, incurring showers of stones from Muslims. The Israeli security force's response included live ammunition, causing injuries and deaths. This incident revived the Intifada and drew some Arab states towards Saddam's standpoint.

Over fifty countries contributed to the allied opposition against Saddam. They forcibly evicted him from Kuwait in Operation Desert Storm, during which time he fired SCUD missiles into Tel Aviv and Haifa. Israel kept to its agreement with America not to retaliate without consultation, but it was made clear to Saddam that if he used chemical weapons, there could be a nuclear response from Israel.

Summary: A people's uprising (Intifada) began late in 1987, raising the PLO's standing enough for them to say they would recognise Israel and declare their own Palestinian state. However, Islamic fundamentalist groups such as Hamas and Islamic Jihad objected and Arafat's PLO reverted to calling for total liberation. The PLO also sided with Iraq in the first Gulf War.

****

14. More Peace Talks

The Gulf War had demonstrated American power, especially given the changes in Russia at the end of the Cold War. The lone super-power now wanted to bring peace to the Middle East and called a conference in Madrid. The PLO, having sided with Iraq, was excluded, but was permitted to choose some members of the Palestinian delegation. Israel attended with some reluctance, and little progress was made. Shamir was still playing for time, especially with the very large rise in immigration into Israel due to the break-up of the Soviet Union. His 'Greater Israel' concept entailed a large increase in Jewish settlements in the West Bank. His opponents believed a Jewish majority in such a Greater Israel was unlikely to happen, therefore the West Bank and Gaza should be released. The 1992 elections in Israel showed that public opinion agreed with this because Labour was returned to power under Yitzak Rabin's leadership.

With the Palestinians intent on self-government in their own state, and Israel intent on keeping control of as much land as possible, it was not surprising that the talks dragged on through several conferences. Frustration at the lack of progress leant support to Hamas, and when Rabin deported four hundred of its activists after the death of an Israeli border policeman, the Arab delegation walked out of the talks. The violence continued and Rabin closed the borders, thereby initiating the separation of Jewish and Palestinian communities. The Madrid talks petered out.

The very limited progress of the Madrid process led Rabin to take the unprecedented step of talking to the PLO directly. The resulting 'Oslo Accord' provided a sequence of events by which Israel would hand over all of the West Bank and Gaza Strip to an elected Palestinian Authority over the next five years. Certain settlements and military installations would remain under Israeli control, as would

Jerusalem. This agreement made significant progress by not having to deal immediately with all aspects of the four most difficult issues, namely the return of Palestinian Arab refugees, Jewish settlements in the occupied territories, water resources and the sovereignty of Jerusalem.

American President Clinton brought Rabin and Arafat to the White House for a famous handshake on September 13th 1993. For the first time, each side recognised the other's nationhood. Arafat confirmed Israel's right to live in peace and security, acceptance of UN Resolutions 242 and 338, and renunciation of terrorism. The Palestinian National Charter was amended accordingly. On the Israeli side, Rabin confirmed recognition of the PLO as the official representative of the Palestinians.

Yasser Arafat returned to Gaza on July 1st 1994 and was elected President of the Palestinian Authority (PA). As has so often been the case when progress has been made, extremists on both sides tried to undermine the new peace process. A Jewish settler gunned down Muslim worshippers at Hebron, while Hamas and Islamic Jihad launched several terrorist attacks. However, these actions failed to prevent the signing of Oslo II, in September 1995, which was the interim agreement on the West Bank and Gaza. It divided the West Bank into three areas: A – Palestinian towns under their own control, B – Palestinian villages under their own civil control but with Israeli security, and C – Israeli settlements under their own control.

Rabin achieved a peace treaty with Jordan in 1994 but the Golan Heights proved to be a stumbling block with Syria. Secret talks with the Palestinians produced the Stockholm Accord in 1995, which offered further progress on the key issues. Then, in November 1995, Rabin was assassinated at a peace rally in Tel Aviv. The culprit was a Jewish right-wing religious Zionist extremist, who wanted to stop the peace progress because of the land concessions. Peres formed a government but declined the Stockholm Accord because he considered the proposals for Jerusalem inadequate and he wanted control of the whole Jordan valley. Apart from this he continued Rabin's programme, but with more emphasis on the economy.

Hamas was gaining popularity due to the delays in the peace process and corruption in the PA. The Israeli assassination of the Hamas suicide bomber mastermind, early in 1996, led to more Hamas attacks, especially bus bombings, and Israeli public opinion moved to the right. An anti-terrorism summit in Egypt, supported by President Clinton and several Arab leaders, was inconclusive, so Peres launched 'Operation Grapes of Wrath' against Hezbollah guerrillas based in South Lebanon in April 1996. The aim was to stop them firing rockets over the border and to send a warning to Syria. However, the invasion caused large numbers of Lebanese to evacuate the region, seriously upsetting their post civil war recovery. The accidental killing of over a hundred refugees in a UN base near Qana brought international protests and an American sponsored cease-fire. The Lebanon campaign, plus the continued terrorist attacks against Israel, resulted in a narrow defeat for Peres by the right wing Binyamin Netanyahu in the 1996 election. This surprised even the Palestinians, whose hopes for an independent state in Gaza and the West Bank would now suffer a setback.

Netanyahu favoured the Greater Israel approach and wanted peace for peace, instead of land for peace. In September 1996 he ordered the opening of a tunnel near the Al-Aksa Mosque in the Old City of Jerusalem, resulting in three days of Arab riots, with casualties. America intervened and Netanyahu eventually made a concession by means of the Hebron Protocol, which divided that city into Jewish and Palestinian zones. It also committed Israel to withdraw from other parts of the West Bank in the next eighteen months.

President Clinton then pressed for progress on Palestinian control of the West Bank in return for better security for Israel. In response, the IDF withdrew from only two per cent of the West Bank, while settlements there continued to grow. Netanyahu also took the last sector of outer Jerusalem by giving the go-ahead for the Har Homa settlement in annexed East Jerusalem. In an attempt to gain some left-wing support, Netanyahu produced the 'Allon Plus' plan, offering forty per cent of the West Bank to the Palestinians. Given that they could expect ninety per cent through Oslo II, the Palestinians turned it down. The Arab states stepped back from normalising relations in the light of the government's change of approach, while Israel accused Arafat of failing to control the extremists.

Netanyahu lost the 1999 election to Labour's Ehud Barak, who decided to pull the IDF out of South Lebanon. The withdrawal became a rout and the South Lebanese Army gave in to Hezbollah, who claimed a great victory for their small Islamic guerrilla force. Barak then turned his attention to the Palestinians and tried to jump straight to final status talks. The preparatory work was done in Stockholm, covering the status of Jerusalem, settlements, borders, water sources and refugees. Arafat and Barak then joined American President Clinton at Camp David on July 11th 2000.

The talks reputedly came close to agreement but eventually failed and recriminations ensued. As various offers and counter-offers did not pass the oral stage, there have been different interpretations of what happened. Barak appeared to offer the Palestinians more than any previous Israeli leader, including the return of some refugees. But, while he may have offered all of Gaza and over ninety per cent of the West Bank, the remaining Jewish settlements and their link roads would have broken up the continuity of the territory. Most observers would agree that Jerusalem in general, and the Temple Mount specifically, were the main stumbling blocks, especially regarding the question of sovereignty. Exactly who would have which parts of the city as their capital, and how were the holy sites to be controlled?

The Israelis felt their concessions since Oslo had been rewarded by suicide bombs and Palestinian inconsistency in tackling the terrorists. The Palestinians had experienced a fall in living standards, exacerbated by border closures, and a loss of hope for a state under their full control. Jewish settlements continued to grow in the West Bank under all the prime ministers in this period. After Camp David therefore, support for the peace process fell away on both sides. The success of Hezbollah in South Lebanon, and Arafat's triumphant return into Gaza, paved the way for another popular uprising.

Summary: After the Gulf War America re-addressed the Arab-Israeli conflict, culminating in the Oslo Accords, signed by Arafat and Rabin in 1993, in which both sides recognised each other's nationhood. Arafat then returned to Gaza and became the PA President, but Rabin was assassinated by a Jewish extremist. Following a period of minimal progress and an Israeli incursion into Lebanon to combat guerrilla attacks, the Americans brought the Arab and Israeli leaders to Camp David in 2000. However, Arafat and Barak failed to reach agreement.

****

15. Another Intifada

The second popular uprising began at the end of September 2000, the Palestinians blaming Ariel Sharon's visit to the Temple Mount. Sharon was making a point, prompted by the Muslim Waqf's (Islamic Authority on the Temple Mount) construction of underground mosques on the site, denying access to archaeologists in order to do so. The visit went off peacefully but the following day, September 30th, rock throwing Palestinians clashed with Israeli riot police at the site. The situation escalated, resulting in the death of four of the demonstrators.

Stones were soon replaced by bullets and human bombs in what became known as the 'Al Aksa Intifada', and casualties grew on both sides. The uprising spread to Galilee where the IDF killed several Israeli Arab protestors, and Jews burned a mosque in Tiberius. Early in 2001 Ariel Sharon became prime minister. Using tanks and bulldozers he besieged Arafat in his Ramallah compound. Despite this action, Arafat retained control over the Intifada by setting up his own Fatah Al Aksa brigade. After Al-Qaeda's 9/11 attack on the World Trade Centre, Israel linked its own battle against terrorism with that of America.

As the Intifada continued, American President George W. Bush sponsored a UN Security Council resolution proposing a Palestinian state. Saudi Crown Prince Abdullah then sponsored an Arab League proposal for normalisation and peaceful relations in return for an Israeli withdrawal to pre-1967 lines. The bombing of a Passover meal in Netanya precluded a diplomatic response from Sharon, who instead authorised counter-terrorism actions, which caused extensive damage to Palestinian infrastructure. During this period part of the town of Jenin was flattened, giving rise to a dispute over casualties. The UN did not find evidence of a massacre but accused both sides of war crimes.

The conflict caused foreign donors to hold back aid to the PA while tourists and investors held back from Israel. This damaged both economies and increased unemployment. Sharon then began expelling foreign workers, in particular those in Israel illegally, but also some others, many of whom worked for international religious organisations. In December 2002, he began erecting a fence or wall along the approximate route of the 'green line' between Israel and the territory occupied during the 1967 war, beginning in the areas where it was most likely to prevent terrorist incursions.

In the second Gulf War, the Palestinians generally backed Saddam Hussein again, hoping that if he won, American influence in the Middle East would decline and Israel would lose support. Despite fears to the contrary, Saddam did not fire missiles at Tel Aviv, so Israel kept out of the conflict. By the end of April 2003, the coalition forces had succeeded in deposing Saddam. Arafat then came under international pressure to relinquish control of the PA because he had backed Saddam. Mahmoud Abbas (Abu Mazen) was appointed prime minister, though Arafat kept the title of president.

After this the Americans launched 'The Road Map', aiming at a final settlement of the Arab-Israeli conflict by 2005. It proposed a two-state solution for peace and security, with an Israeli withdrawal from the West Bank, Gaza and East Jerusalem. The PA had to clearly accept Israel's right to exist, deal with terrorist groups, and reform their institutions. Israel had to commit to a Palestinian state, end violence and demolition of houses, freeze settlement construction - dismantling those built since March 2001, and progressively withdraw from areas occupied during the Intifada. A 'quartet' consisting of the US, UN, Russia and the European Union, would monitor progress.

Terrorist attacks occurred in Israel, aimed at de-railing the Road Map, and these brought Israeli strikes on terrorist leaders. Arafat managed to maintain control despite the imposition of Mahmoud Abbas as prime minister. The UN Security Council had given its support to the Road Map in November 2003 but, in the same month, Sharon announced his own plans for disengagement from Palestinian territories should the Road Map fail to end the ongoing terrorism. Yossi Beilin and Yasser Abed Rabbo then produced the Geneva Accord peace plan, which attempted to solve the Jerusalem problems which had dogged Camp David in 2000. It was a good example of what can be achieved by the active moderates on both sides. It proposed two states, with East and West Jerusalem as capitals. Regarding the troublesome problem of sovereignty, the Palestinians would get the Temple Mount and most of the Old City; the Israelis would get the Jewish Quarter of the Old City and the Western Wall.

Unfortunately, the extremists had other ideas and 2004 saw the continuation of suicide attacks against Israeli citizens and the assassination of Hamas leaders, including their spiritual leader Sheikh Yassin, by Israeli forces. The International Court of Justice ruled against the ever-lengthening Israeli security wall, or fence, while Sharon sought backing for his disengagement plans.

Yasser Arafat died of natural causes in November 2004 and Mahmoud Abbas became President of the Palestinian Authority in January 2005. Sharon formed a national unity government which passed his disengagement plans. He also met with Egyptian President Mubarak and King Abdullah in Jordan, where they announced an end to violence, thus closing the Intifada. At a conference in Cairo, Islamic Jihad and Hamas leaders joined the PLO in suspending attacks against Israelis. Israel pulled out of Jericho a week later. Despite this, the suicide bombing and Israeli reprisals resumed in the summer. The Gaza Strip was closed, prior to the removal of all Jewish settlers in mid-August, 2005. The disengagement was completed by early September and Gaza was handed over to the PA. Sharon then addressed the UN, calling for peace and an end to terrorism. He recognised Palestinian rights but asserted Israel's right to a united Jerusalem.

Summary: The second popular uprising (Intifada) began in 2000 and was more violent than its predecessor. Terrorism and counter-terrorism measures limited responses to outside peace proposals. After the Second Gulf War the Americans' Road Map plan was put forward. Meetings between the region's leaders and a cease-fire with Hamas, ended the Intifada in 2005. Israel then withdrew from the Gaza Strip, handing it over to the PA, led by Mahmoud Abbas, following the death of Yasser Arafat.

****

16. Complications

Sharon's problems with his own Likud party led him to form a new, less right-wing 'Kadima' party. In January 2006 he then suffered a stroke which left him in a coma, and the Kadima party in the hands of Ehud Olmert. A few days later there was an unexpected result in the Palestinian Legislative Council elections when Hamas defeated Fatah. The main reason quoted for this outcome was that of corruption in the PA led by Fatah. Because Hamas refused to recognise Israel, their coming to power threatened to damage hopes for peace in the Holy Land at a time when progress was being made. Their stance cost them much international aid, so they resorted to smuggling money and arms across Gaza's border with Egypt. They also continued firing rockets at Sderot, the nearest Israeli town to Gaza, incurring targeted killings by the Israeli forces.

PA President Mahmoud Abbas persevered with the matter of national unity in the West Bank and Gaza, and the right of return for refugees. At the same time, the IDF invaded Gaza to try and stop the rockets and rescue a captured soldier, Gilad Schalit. They failed to find him and matters deteriorated when Hezbollah, by this time very much a surrogate for Iran, captured two Israeli soldiers in the north. They followed up with a rocket attack, after which Israeli forces moved into South Lebanon. The IDF used heavy artillery and aircraft against targets inside Lebanon, causing thousands of civilians to leave their homes. Hezbollah came back with rockets reaching as far as Haifa and Tiberius. As the situation escalated, the UN Security Council brought about a cease-fire on August 14th. After this, the remainder of 2006 saw little progress.

Early in 2007, Israeli excavations at the Temple Mount alarmed the Arab world - an indication of the sensitivity attached to anything that happens on that holy site. A meeting in Mecca then tried to persuade Hamas and Fatah to share power. A trial run did not last and in June Hamas attacked Fatah, throwing them out of the Gaza Strip. Abbas immediately dissolved the unity government, with backing from Egypt and Jordan. The official PA then became based in the West Bank, with a new prime minister. Hamas, led by Haniyeh, was left in charge of Gaza, where the humanitarian position worsened due to the international boycott of Hamas (due to their refusal to recognise Israel). Later in the year, the Americans convened a peace conference at Annapolis which resulted in a return to the Road Map, with the intention of completing the agreement by the end of 2008.

Meanwhile a new Islamic factor was coming to the fore as Iranian President Ahmadinejad made provocative anti-Israel pronouncements. The western world also believed he was developing nuclear weapons and UN sanctions were imposed. If matters on the Israeli-Palestinian front were making little or no progress, the wider Islamic situation was not going to help much. Both Hezbollah and Hamas were drawing support from Iran.

Early in 2008 Hamas breached the barrier between Gaza and Egypt, causing thousands of Gazans to spill over into their neighbour's country, as well as allowing traffic in the opposite direction. When Egypt restored the barrier, smuggling of arms through tunnels continued and became an ongoing problem for the Israelis. In addition, there were attempts to get arms into Gaza by sea.

June of that year saw a truce between Israel and Hamas, but the rivalry between Hamas and Fatah continued in earnest. Fatah arrested Hamas activists in the West Bank while Hamas arrested Fatah members in Gaza. While this continued, Israel had no clear guidance on which party to negotiate with.

November 2008 saw Barak Obama elected as the new American president and he took a keen interest in the Middle East from the word go. The Quartet reaffirmed the Annapolis decision to return to the Road Map. However, in mid December Hamas announced that the truce with Israel was over and resumed the firing of rockets from Gaza to the nearest Israeli town of Sderot, and even beyond. The

Israeli response was Operation Cast Lead, in which the IDF fired their artillery into Gaza to try and knock out the rocket launchers as well as Hamas command and control positions. There were civilian deaths which would lead to accusations against Israel by way of the Goldstone enquiry later in the year. However, as Goldstone himself later admitted, he did not receive all the relevant facts at the time of his enquiry.

The elections in Israel in January 2009 saw a move to the right and Binyamin Netanyahu began his second spell as prime minister. The American President maintained his interest in the Middle East and exerted pressure on Netanyahu during a speech made in Cairo. Obama called for an end to Israeli settlement building in the West Bank and for Arab recognition of Israel, which would serve to return the situation to a position which had previously existed. In response, Netanyahu accepted the need to create a Palestinian state and later put a temporary freeze on building in the West Bank.

Meanwhile the Iranians re-elected Ahmadinejad, although there was serious opposition to him this time. As well as coming under international criticism for its repression of that opposition, Iran was also coming under increasing pressure regarding the purpose of its nuclear development, especially when a secret factory was revealed. As far as the Israelis were concerned, not only would Hezbollah and Hamas continue to receive Iranian backing, but there was the increasing threat of Iran producing nuclear-headed missiles and firing them at targets in Israel.

The Hamas – Fatah stalemate limited Palestinian progress, and that with the next general election due in January 2010. In August 2009 Fatah held its first congress for many years. The PA stated that it would declare a state unilaterally within two years, but by November Mahmoud Abbas was saying he would not stand for re-election due to the lack of progress in negotiations. Then he said he would postpone the general election because it would be impossible to arrange in Gaza, and that would cut out far too many people.

In May 2010 the Free Gaza Movement and a Turkish Human Rights group sent a flotilla of ships to try and break Israel's blockade of Gaza – set up to prevent weapons being smuggled in. Israeli Special Forces met resistance when boarding the largest of the ships and killed nine Turkish activists. Following this, President Obama, amongst others, put pressure on Israel to moderate their blockade, which they did. Israel's concerns about weapons on their doorstep remained, however, and the UN increased the sanctions on Iran because of their nuclear programme.

The Autumn of 2010 saw the beginning of talks between Israel and the PA. To expand the time for these talks, President Obama put pressure on Israel to extend its temporary freeze on settlement construction in the West Bank. Netanyahu declined, so the PA walked out of the talks, leaving a frustrated American president. In January 2011, Al Jazeera news station released the 'Palestinian Papers' which indicated that the PA had been willing to make significant concessions to Israel during their talks.

Late in January, Lebanon's Saad Hariri was replaced by Najib Mikati of Hezbollah, but a much greater wind of change was about to sweep through several countries in the Middle East. Popular pro-democracy uprisings against long-serving – or dominating – leaders, arose in Tunisia, Yemen, Libya, Syria and, most significantly, Egypt. In this so-called 'Arab Spring' the internet and mobile phones played a key role in bringing large crowds onto the streets, co-ordinating their efforts and transmitting news to the rest of the world. Peaceful demonstrations were met by varying degrees of force.

Hosni Mubarak eventually stood down in Egypt, leaving the army in charge until elections could be held in the summer of 2011. Gaddafi resisted in Libya, incurring NATO support for the rebels. Assad resisted in Syria, where large numbers of demonstrators were reported dead or injured.

The KEY PLAYERS in 2011

The QUARTET:
United Nations
European Community
Russia and USA -
(President Barak Obama)

TURKEY
Tayip Erdogan
Prime Minister

IRAN
Mahmoud Ahmadinejad
Prime Minister -- backs
Hamas & Hezbollah

LEBANON
Najib Mikati
Prime Minister

HEZBOLLAH
Based in S. Lebanon

Beirut

Damascus

SYRIA
Bashir Assad
President

Golan Heights

State of ISRAEL
Binyamin Netanyahu
Prime Minister

Haifa

Sea of Galilee

WEST BANK
Mahmoud Abbas
Fatah Party.
Palestinian Authority
President

Tel Aviv

Ramallah

Amman

Jerusalem

Gaza City

GAZA
Ismail Haniyeh
Hamas Party
Prime Minister

Dead Sea

The
Negev

JORDAN
Abdullah bin al-Hussain
King

EGYPT
Interim control by
Army after
Mubarak deposed

Eilat

Aqaba

SAUDI ARABIA
Abdullah bin Abdul Aziz Al-Saud
King and Prime Minister

As the Arab Spring continued, Hamas and the PA agreed a reconciliation in late April, with a general election to come in the autumn. At the beginning of May they issued a demand for a Palestinian State, based on the pre-1967 borders. Egypt now backed this demand (Mubarak had not done so). When Obama showed his support, Netanyahu made it quite clear that the 1967 borders were indefensible. There were further issues for the Israelis, namely that Hamas had still not recognised Israel's right to exist, and that Islamic groups such as the Muslim Brotherhood could gain more influence in Egypt. Generally speaking, the pressure for a two-state solution was increasing.

Summary: Hamas defeated Fatah in the PA general election thereby producing a dilemma for Israel. The comparatively moderate PA under Abbas was restricted to the West Bank. The more militant Hamas would not recognise Israel and so lost international support. However, they received support instead from the Islamic regime in Iran. America's new president began exerting pressure in the region. Pro-democracy movements in several Arab countries and a reconciliation between Hamas and the PA increased the pressure on Israel for a two-state solution.

****

17. Recognition and Rockets

In the Autumn of 2011, PA President Abbas launched a bid for full membership of the UN; an action sometimes referred to as the 'Palestinian Spring'. An initial success saw Palestine become the 195th member of UNESCO – United Nations Educational, Scientific, and Cultural Organisation. The American response was to cut $70 million of its annual contribution to that organisation. This was a reminder that a bid for Palestinian statehood would bring a US veto at the UN Security Council, through whom such a bid would have to proceed. Furthermore, the UK and France were likely show a lack of support by abstaining. By-passing the Security Council and going direct to the UN General Assembly could only bring enhanced observer status at best, so the PA held back for the time being. Instead, the UN, along with European Community, Russia and the US, pressed for a resumption of peace talks. Exploratory talks took place in Jordan in January 2012 but soon failed. The Palestinians were first demanding a halt to settlement construction on occupied land, while Israel refused to accept any pre-conditions to the resumption of full talks.

By now Israel had set up its 'Iron Dome' air defence system, which was successful in intercepting most (but not all) of the rockets directed into Israel by Hamas in Gaza and Hezbollah in Lebanon. Despite this, the rocket attacks continued during 2012, their range, though not their accuracy, extending to Tel Aviv and Jerusalem. In November, Israel launched 'Operation Pillar of Defence' to deter rocket fire from Gaza. There were air strikes but no ground invasion, despite the appearance of tanks. The recently elected President Morsi of Egypt brokered a cease-fire.

Earlier in the year Israeli Prime Minister Netanyahu avoided early elections by forming a unity government with the centrist Kadima party. This strengthened his hand in opposing Iran's development of nuclear power – increasingly seen as the main threat to Israel. The deal with Kadima included a pledge to review the situation regarding the stalled peace talks. The PA meanwhile continued to pursue recognition by the UN. Early in November 2012 it submitted a draft resolution for international recognition of a state in the West Bank, Gaza and Jerusalem, plus an upgrade from its present status at the UN to 'non-member observer'. Israel threatened to cancel the Oslo Accords if the second of these was accepted. The UN response came on November 29th, the sixty-fifth anniversary of resolution 181 (the 1947 UN Partition Plan, see page 61), accepting the non-member observer status by 138 to 9 votes, with 38 abstentions. Israel responded by approving more housing on land between Jerusalem and Maale Adumim.

In the general election at the beginning of 2013, Netanyahu lost ground to the new centre-left and ultra-nationalist parties, but still formed a coalition government. Peace talks resumed in Washington DC, following the release of over a hundred Palestinian prisoners. A two-state solution remained the aim.

2013 saw some significant changes in countries surrounding Israel. Within months of his election success, Egypt's President Morsi, of the Muslim Brotherhood, was soon making moves to appropriate more power to his position. This led to mass demonstrations and his removal from power by the army after only one year in office. General Sisi led the coup and went on to win a general election the following year after resigning his military status.

While there was no obvious Arab Spring in Jordan, that country did begin to receive large numbers of refugees from the worsening Syrian conflict. Iran was backing Syria and both of them were backing Hezbollah in Lebanon, hence the persistent threat of rockets into Israel from that direction. But, the civil war between Syrian's President Bashir Assad and the various rebel groups, was causing considerable suffering and destruction in his country, hence the exodus of people to Jordan, and to Turkey, Lebanon and Iraq. Given that the Western nations were keeping out of the region as far as sending in troops was concerned, something of a vacuum arose. It was filled in early 2014 by the formation of ISIL, (or IS), the Islamic State in the Levant. 'Daesh' is the Arabic name. The originators adhered to the fundamentalist Salafi Jihadist doctrine of Sunni Islam. They first drove the Iraqis out of key cities, including Mosul, and then, in June 2014, declared a 'World-Wide Caliphate of Islam' covering parts of Iraq and Syria. In so doing, they declared authority over all Muslims. Being Sunni Muslims, they were opposed to the Shi'ite Muslims rulers of Iran and Syria. Their extreme acts of violence brought an American led international intervention the same year. It would take four years to remove them from the region and end their caliphate, but their ideology remained intact.

The above drew a lot of attention away from the Holy Land situation during 2014. Hamas and Fatah tried to form a unity government and the US tried to get peace talks underway again, but both of these failed to meet the set deadlines for progress. Then, in July, tensions rose following the kidnapping and killing of three Israeli teenagers in the West Bank, and the suspected revenge killing of an Arab youth in East Jerusalem. Large numbers of rockets were launched from Gaza, and Israel responded with Operation Protective Edge, which threatened a ground invasion of Gaza. A major conflict ensued for seven weeks, with a high casualty rate. Once again it was Egypt who brokered the ceasefire, in late August. Hamas retained control inside Gaza. Israel and Egypt would control the blockade, with the former easing imports, especially reconstruction materials, and doubling the fishing zone to 6 km.

With regard to reconstruction materials, there was some concern that a quantity of these would be directed to the repair and extension of tunnels. Since taking over in Gaza, Hamas had developed a system of tunnels inside Gaza for the storage of weapons. They also built tunnels under the border fence into Israel, thereby causing concern among local Israeli citizens who feared for their safety. Over time, the tunnels became more and more sophisticated, so Israel had to become more and more vigilant and innovative in its detection of them.

2014 ended with a UN Security Council vote on Palestinian statehood, on December 30th. Voting was 8 to 5 in favour, with 2 abstentions, thus falling short of the two-thirds majority required. Israel's security needs were not adequately met and there was no need for a US veto.

The PA received a boost in May 2015 when the Vatican recognised the Palestinian State, switching its support from the PLO, (Palestinian Liberation Organisation). Netanyahu had earlier stated his rejection of the two-state solution, should he be re-elected that Spring. He was, but his new coalition government had only a tiny majority. Violence escalated in the Autumn of 2015 when the Israeli defence minister banned Muslim activists meeting on the Temple Mount to shout abuse and intimidate Jewish visitors. This sparked violence on the Temple Mount and in the adjacent Muslim Quarter of the Old City. President Abbas backed the activists and renewed the PA's claim to Jerusalem. One of the key issues, sovereignty over Jerusalem and its holy places, had come to the fore once again.

There was a significant change in Turkey during 2016. A failed coup against President Erdogan gave him cause to purge any opposition he could find. As a rule, Turkey had a secular government, but Erdogan seemed to be developing the idea of establishing a caliphate with himself as its caliph. Would this include the Holy Land in due time?

Finally, back to the UN in December 2016. The Security Council passed a motion condemning Israeli settlements on occupied land. The motion passed because the US abstained, rather than use its veto. This, in effect, was an unprecedented rebuke from the American Obama government, which said it was only following the line set out by President Reagan many years previously. However, the American general election in November 2016 was to change everything.

Summary: In the five-year period from late 2011, the Palestinians aimed to improve their status by recourse to the United Nations. Violence centred mainly on rockets from Hamas in Gaza and the Israeli responses to that. Israel's growing security concern, was Iran; its development of nuclear power and threats against the Holy Land.

****

18. Expect the Unexpected

Donald Trump had not been expected to win the American general election, but the opinion polls were proved wrong (again.) He took office in January 2017. The following month the US announced that it was open to the idea of a one state solution – a major shift in policy. Israel indicated its future intent by retroactively legalising 4000 settler homes in the West Bank, and, soon afterwards the US appointed a new ambassador who was known to be supportive of settlements. Russia responded by restating its support for a two-state solution. In addition, President Putin moved away from advocating international control over Jerusalem to having East Jerusalem as capital of Palestine and West Jerusalem as capital of Israel. Hamas also changed policy by stating that they would accept an interim Palestinian state using pre – 1967 borders, but fell short of acknowledging Israel's right to exist.

Another unexpected move came at the end of 2017 when President Trump announced the American recognition of Jerusalem as the capital of Israel, and ordered his embassy to move there from Tel Aviv. The new embassy opened in May 2018 accompanied by Palestinian protests. The chosen date was the anniversary of Israel's independence, and the corresponding Palestinian Nakba (Catastrophe). Two months later, the Knesset passed laws declaring Israel a Jewish state, with Hebrew as its official language and Jerusalem as its undivided capital.

President Trump had appointed his son-in-law, Jared Kushner (of Jewish descent), to head up the push for a peace plan. At the same time, he threatened to reduce American aid to the Palestinians if they failed to take part in talks. By the end of 2018 he had stopped funding UNWRA (the UN agency for Palestinian refugees), and cut millions of dollars of direct US Aid to Palestinian causes. Continued non-participation by the PA led to Trump closing the PLO Mission in Washington and revoking the envoy's visas. During 2019 the US made further policy reversals by recognising Israel's annexation of the Golan Heights, and withdrawing its legal view that Israeli settlements in Palestinian territories violated international law. There was an international conference in Manama, Bahrain, to consider the economic aspects of the American peace plan for the Middle East but the PA did not attend. Kushner challenged them to think again.

Meanwhile Prime Minister Netanyahu was running into difficulties on the home front. He had been under investigation since late 2016 for accepting bribes, fraud, and breach of trust. This did not help him in the general election of April 2019. In addition, the Ultra-Orthodox Jewish politicians, who normally joined his coalition government, were resisting calls for conscription into army service. Their strong preference was for their young men to study Torah and Talmud in the yeshivas (bible schools) – hence avoiding three years in the army, and living off the state. As a result, Netanyahu failed to get a coalition, but did manage to dissolve the Knesset and try again in September. At that election, his Likud party won 35 seats, the same as Benny Gantz's Blue and White party. With the Ultra-Orthodox still concerned about conscription and Gantz unhappy about Netanyahu's corruption charges, neither of them could form a coalition (61 minimum required), and a third general election was set for March 2020. To achieve this, the Knesset voted to dissolve itself for the first time in its history!

Netanyahu (by now Israel's longest serving prime minister) was indicted in January 2020 on the charges mentioned above, but the law allowed him to continue as prime minister. The general election two months later was another stalemate, but the public had had enough and the situation in the country demanded a positive outcome. A coalition government was formed, with a rotation of the premiership – Netanyahu first, with Gantz, due to take over in November 2021.

Apart from having three general elections in under a year, the Israeli public were concerned about the latest unexpected event. The Covid-19 virus had originated in China in the Autumn of 2019, and spread around the world at an alarming rate. Israel's first case was diagnosed on February 21st 2020. Within a month Netanyahu had introduced legal enforcement of restrictions on public activity and movement, making it one of the first countries to 'lockdown'. It would also be one of the first to introduce a second lockdown – in September that year.

One of the first measures against Covid-19 was to impose a fourteen day quarantine on people flying into the country. Given that driving into the country was not an option, this action was comparatively easy to augment, so it quickly had a significant effect on tourism. 2019 had been the third consecutive year in which Israel's tourism broke the previous record, reaching a considerable 4.55 million. Now, suddenly, the hotels emptied and the Holy Land sites became deserted. The economy would take a serious hit.

This writer was in the country during March 2020 and witnessed the change in the Galilee region. However, there was some good news, namely the rainfall during the winter months. By mid-March the Sea of Galilee was close to being full for the first time in many years. While Eilat, in the far south of the country, had the use of a water desalination plant from the 1970's, additional plants were not built until after the turn of the century, when the authorities eventually accepted that the annual rainfall was not going to provide sufficient supplies to meet all requirements. The regular addition of new plants has been aimed at providing drinking water and hence reducing demands on the Sea of Galilee. There are aquifers which supply some of the country's water, but they had also been seriously depleted by years of low rainfall. The Dead Sea was lower than ever because it had not been topped up by any surplus from Galilee. A project with Jordan to feed water in from the Red Sea continued to be talked about, and maybe came a little closer, but there was no sign of work getting underway.

If climate change was causing more erratic weather, it was at least providing more precipitation for a country with a growing population. Water resources had always been a major issue for the Holy Land, especially in the light of the Israeli-Palestinian conflict, but the situation had eased for the time being at least. The census of 2020 reported a population of over nine million, which was over ten times that in 1948 when Israel declared its independence. The increase included 3.3 million immigrants over the seventy-two year period. The breakdown of the population stood at 74% Jewish, 21% Arab and 5% other, including Druze. The Arab population was mostly Muslim, with other Arabs constituting most of the country's 2% of Christians. Of the total world Jewish population, 47% were living in Israel. These figures were for the State of Israel. Figures from 2017 for the West Bank reported nearly two and three-quarter million Arabs and 380,000 Jewish settlers. The same census reported one and three-quarter million Arabs living in Gaza.

Arguably the most unexpected events of 2020 came in the Autumn. The Abraham Accords, normalising relations between the United Arab Emirates (UAE) and Israel, were signed at the White House on September 15th. Bahrain followed suit on October 18th, in a ceremony in that country's capital, Manama. A few days later Sudan began normalising relations with Israel. The Americans had offered the UAE advanced weapons, such as the F35 jet fighter, and Netanyahu had agreed to suspend his recently stated intention to annexe parts of the West Bank. The reason for these Arab countries making such a move was due to their having a serious concern in common with Israel, namely the threat from Iran. While Iran is Shi'ite Muslim, the others are Sunni (see page 26). Iran was backing rebels in Yemen as well as backing Hamas and Hezbollah, as previously mentioned. Furthermore, many doubted its stated purpose of developing nuclear power solely for domestic purposes. Back in

2015, an accord had been reached between Iran and five western powers (UK, US, France, Germany, Russia) plus China. Under this arrangement, Iran would limit its nuclear activities and re-admit international inspection of its facilities, in return for the lifting of international sanctions which had been seriously affecting the country's economy. President Trump pulled out of the agreement in August 2018, citing Iranian violations, and he re-imposed sanctions.

The Palestinians protested the Abraham Accords, burning the UAE flag alongside the Israeli flag. However, along with Egypt (since 1979) and Jordan (since 1994), there were now five Arab countries at peace with Israel, with the prospect of more to follow. The saying, 'the enemy of my enemy is my friend' fits this situation. The Shi'ite versus Sunni fight for control over Islam in the region aligned Israel with many of its (Sunni) Arab neighbours. Iran's stated intention of destroying Israel caused many to suspect it was secretly developing a nuclear weapon. Its backing of Hamas and Hezbollah was probably damaging support for the Palestinian cause from other countries.

Summary: The US under Trump recognised Jerusalem as Israel's capital and moved its embassy there from Tel Aviv. It put pressure on the Palestinians to take part in peace talks by cutting aid if they declined. It also brokered peace deals between three Arab states and Israel, taking advantage of Sunni Muslim concerns over the Iranian Shi'ite Muslim nuclear threat – one shared by Israel. The Covid-19 virus brought Holy Land tourism to a halt, but the exceptionally wet weather restored the water reserves for a population passing the nine million mark.

****

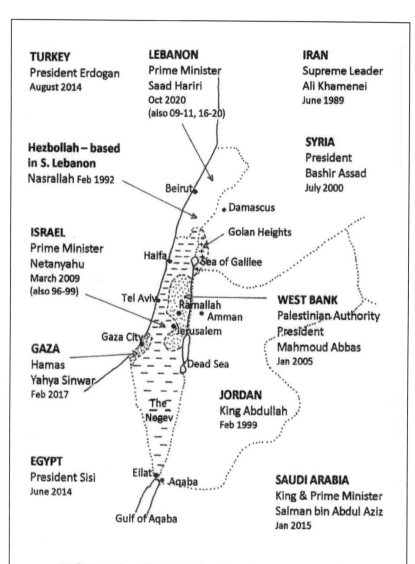

TURKEY
President Erdogan
August 2014

**Hezbollah – based
in S. Lebanon**
Nasrallah Feb 1992

ISRAEL
Prime Minister
Netanyahu
March 2009
(also 96-99)

GAZA
Hamas
Yahya Sinwar
Feb 2017

EGYPT
President Sisi
June 2014

LEBANON
Prime Minister
Saad Hariri
Oct 2020
(also 09-11, 16-20)

Beirut

Damascus

Golan Heights

Haifa

Sea of Galilee

Tel Aviv

Ramallah

Amman

Jerusalem

Gaza City

Dead Sea

The
Negev

Eilat

Aqaba

Gulf of Aqaba

IRAN
Supreme Leader
Ali Khamenei
June 1989

SYRIA
President
Bashir Assad
July 2000

WEST BANK
Palestinian Authority
President
Mahmoud Abbas
Jan 2005

JORDAN
King Abdullah
Feb 1999

SAUDI ARABIA
King & Prime Minister
Salman bin Abdul Aziz
Jan 2015

AROUND the HOLY LAND at the beginning of 2021
With date of leaders' coming to power.

Epilogue

This short history has shown how three major world religions came to have holy sites in a small area of land in the Middle East. The geographical location of this piece of land, a bridge between continents, made it an important place to control or influence. After Babylonians, Medes & Persians, Greeks, Romans, Ummayad and Abbasid Muslims, Crusaders, Mamelukes and Ottomans, came European and American involvement.

The Jewish people fleeing the Russian pogroms in the 1880s returned to their biblical homeland in numbers large enough to provoke Arab nationalism and the modern-day conflict emerged. After the British Mandate failed to solve the problem, the United Nations took over and the new State of Israel came into being in 1948. Full scale wars between Jews and Arabs were followed by two popular uprisings while the major powers tried to bring peace to the region. Most recently, some Arab states have normalised relations with Israel in opposition to the Iranian regime which threatens control of the whole region. At times there have been positive, forward moves in the peace process, only for the extremists, which there are on both sides, to intervene and limit, or even reverse, that progress.

The Holy Land continues to draw tourists from all over the world, with record numbers in recent years, until the Covid pandemic intervened. Life goes on through the difficulties, albeit with its ups and downs, while the those beyond its borders seek to resolve its problems.

****

Time-Line Summary

(The earliest few dates are estimates)

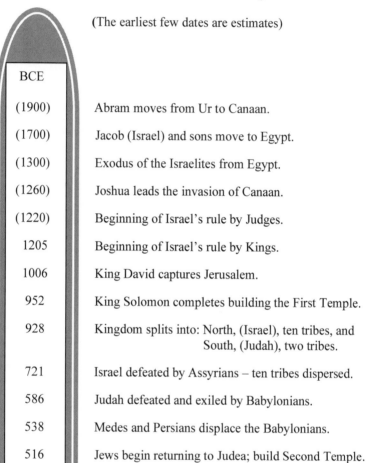

BCE	
(1900)	Abram moves from Ur to Canaan.
(1700)	Jacob (Israel) and sons move to Egypt.
(1300)	Exodus of the Israelites from Egypt.
(1260)	Joshua leads the invasion of Canaan.
(1220)	Beginning of Israel's rule by Judges.
1205	Beginning of Israel's rule by Kings.
1006	King David captures Jerusalem.
952	King Solomon completes building the First Temple.
928	Kingdom splits into: North, (Israel), ten tribes, and South, (Judah), two tribes.
721	Israel defeated by Assyrians – ten tribes dispersed.
586	Judah defeated and exiled by Babylonians.
538	Medes and Persians displace the Babylonians.
516	Jews begin returning to Judea; build Second Temple.
332	Greek Empire takes control of the Holy Land.
167	Maccabean revolt against the Greeks.
63	Roman Empire takes control of the Holy Land.

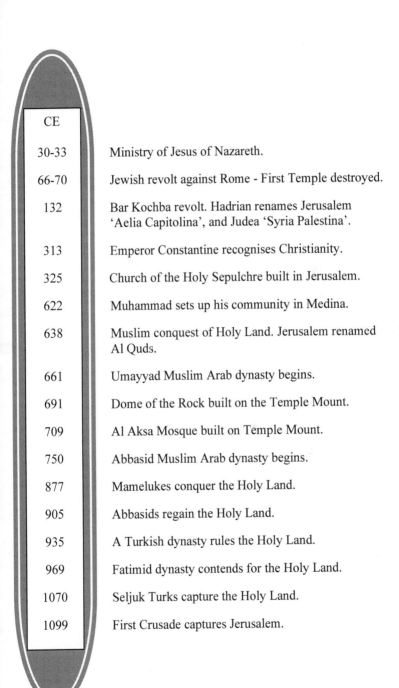

CE	
30-33	Ministry of Jesus of Nazareth.
66-70	Jewish revolt against Rome - First Temple destroyed.
132	Bar Kochba revolt. Hadrian renames Jerusalem 'Aelia Capitolina', and Judea 'Syria Palestina'.
313	Emperor Constantine recognises Christianity.
325	Church of the Holy Sepulchre built in Jerusalem.
622	Muhammad sets up his community in Medina.
638	Muslim conquest of Holy Land. Jerusalem renamed Al Quds.
661	Umayyad Muslim Arab dynasty begins.
691	Dome of the Rock built on the Temple Mount.
709	Al Aksa Mosque built on Temple Mount.
750	Abbasid Muslim Arab dynasty begins.
877	Mamelukes conquer the Holy Land.
905	Abbasids regain the Holy Land.
935	A Turkish dynasty rules the Holy Land.
969	Fatimid dynasty contends for the Holy Land.
1070	Seljuk Turks capture the Holy Land.
1099	First Crusade captures Jerusalem.

105

1187	Saladin takes Jerusalem from the Crusaders.
1291	Mamelukes expel last Crusaders from the Holy Land.
1517	Ottomans take control of the Holy Land.
1801	Napoleon fails to conquer the Holy Land.
1831-40	Muhammad Ali rules Holy Land for Ottoman Sultan.
1839	British Consulate opens in Jerusalem.
1842	First Protestant Bishop of Jerusalem.
1843	First Zionist writings by Jewish Rabbis.
1850	E. Orthodox and R. Catholic disputes over holy sites.
1861	First warning, by Ahad Ha'am, of potential for Arab-Jewish conflict in the Holy Land.
1881	Assassination of Russian Czar leads to first Jewish aliyah to the Holy Land.
1886-92	First disputes and civil unrest between Arabs & Jews.
1896	Herzl's book. 'The Jewish State'.
1905	Beginning of second Jewish Aliyah.
1909	Young Turks revolution.
1914-18	World War I. Arab revolt against Ottoman Turks.
1917	Balfour Declaration. Allenby captures Jerusalem Bolshevik revolution in Russia.
1920	San Remo conference partitions Ottoman lands.

1923	Official start of British Mandate in Palestine.
1936	Arab revolt against the Mandate.
1939-45	World War II.
1947	UN Resolution 181 ends British Mandate and recommends partition.
May 1948	Israel declares independence and goes on to win the ensuing war with its Arab neighbours.
May 1964	Palestinian Liberation Organisation established.
Jun 1967	Six-Day War. Israel captures East Jerusalem.
Sep 1970	King Hussein expels the PLO from Jordan.
Oct 1973	Yom Kippur War.
Sep 1978	Camp David Peace Conference.
Jan 1979	Islamic Revolution in Iran.
May 1979	Egypt-Israel Peace Treaty.
Jun 1981	Israel bombs Iraqi nuclear reactor at Osirak.
Apr 1982	Israel completes withdrawal from Sinai.
Jun 1982	Operation Peace for Galilee in Southern Lebanon.
Dec 1987	Outbreak of First Intifada (Popular Uprising).
Nov 1988	Declaration of Palestinian independence.
Jan 1991	First Gulf War.

Oct 1991	Madrid Peace Conference begins.
Sep 1993	Oslo Peace Accords.
May 1994	Jericho and Gaza handed over to the Palestinian Authority (PA) by Israel.
Jul 1994	Yasser Arafat elected PA President.
Nov 1995	Assassination of Prime Minister Rabin.
Apr 1996	Operation Grapes of Wrath in South Lebanon.
Feb 1999	Abdullah succeeds Hussein as King of Jordan.
Mar 2000	Pope John Paul II visits Israel.
Jul 2000	Camp David peace talks failure.
Sep 2000	Onset of Second Intifada (Popular Uprising).
Dec 2002	Israel begins building fence/wall around W Bank.
Mar 2003	Second Gulf War.
Apr 2003	American Road Map introduced.
Nov 2004	Mahmoud Abbas succeeds Yasser Arafat.
Sep 2005	Israel hands over Gaza Strip to PA control.
Jan 2007	Hamas ejects Fatah from Gaza.
Dec 2008	Operation Cast Lead by IDF against Gaza.
May 2010	Israel intercepts flotilla from Turkey to Gaza.
Sep 2010	Failure of Israel – PA talks.

Feb 2011	Onset of Arab Spring, pro-democracy Movement. Mubarak stands down in Egypt
May 2011	PA/Hamas call for state based on pre-1967 borders.
Sep 2011	Abbas launches bid for full UN membership.
Oct 2011	Palestine becomes full member of UNESCO. Israel sets up Iron Dome defence system.
Jan 2012	Jordan hosts peace talks but without any progress.
Nov 2012	IDF Operation Pillar of Defence v Hamas in Gaza. Palestine given non-member observer status at UN
July 2013	Peace Talks resume in Washington DC. President Morsi deposed by General Sisi in Egypt.
Jun 2014	Israel's Operation Protective Edge v Hamas. ISIL declares Worldwide Caliphate of Islam.
Dec 2014	UN Security Council vote on Palestinian state fails to get the required two-thirds majority.
May 2015	Vatican recognises Palestinian state.
Dec 2016	UN Security Council condemns Israeli settlements on occupied land as US abstains from vote.
Jan 2017	US under Trump open to one state solution.
Dec 2017	US recognises Jerusalem as capital of Israel.
May 2018	US embassy opens in Jerusalem.
Jul 2018	Knesset declares Israel a Jewish state, Jerusalem undivided capital, and Hebrew official language.

Aug 2018	US cuts aid to Palestinians due to their non-Participation in peace talks.
Mar 2019	US recognises Israel's annexation of Golan.
Jun 2019	Economic part of peace plan talks in Bahrain.
Sep 2019	Second failure (with April) to form next Knesset.
Mar 2020	Coronavirus pandemic puts a halt on three record years of tourism to the Holy Land.
Mar 2020	Third general election in a year in Israel leads to a coalition with alternating prime ministers.
May 2020	First stage in Netanyahu trial following indictment for corruption in 2016.
Sep 2020	Normalisation of relations – Israel & UAE, the Abraham Accords.
Oct 2020	Normalisation of relations – Israel & Bahrain. Sudan begins normalisation of relations.
Jan 2021	Trump's Republican administration replaced by Biden and Democrats.
Feb 2021	Israel's advanced covid vaccination programme raises hope of early end to lockdown.
Mar 2021	The fourth General election in Israel in two years indicates little change from the previous three.

League of Nations San Remo Resolution 1920

"The Mandatory will be responsible for putting into effect the declaration originally made on November 8, 1917, by the British Government, and adopted by the other Allied Powers, in favour of the establishment in Palestine of a national home for the Jewish people, it being clearly understood that nothing shall be done which may prejudice the civil and religious rights of the existing non-Jewish communities in Palestine, or the rights and political status enjoyed by Jews in any other country."

United Nations (UN) Resolutions

181   Adopted 29/11/1947: recommended the end of the British Mandate of Palestine and the division of the land into Jewish and Arab states, with the Jerusalem-Bethlehem area under international protection overseen by the UN.

242   Adopted 22/11/1967 by the UN Security Council: required the establishing of a just and lasting peace n the Middle East, to include withdrawal of Israel armed forces from territories occupied in the recent conflict (Six Day War) and, termination of all claims or states of belligerency and respect for and acknowledgement of the sovereignty, territorial integrity and political independence of every State in the area and their right to live in peace within secure and recognised boundaries free from threats or acts of force.

338   Adopted 22/10/1973 by the UN Security Council: called for a cease fire in the 1973 (Yom Kippur) war within twelve hours of the adoption of the proposal. The resolution came from a joint proposal by the USA and Russia and it helped establish the framework for a conference in Geneva in the December of that year.

UPDATES SPACE